THE CASE FOR
Grace

• STUDENT EDITION •

Also by Lee Strobel:

THE CASE FOR
Grace
• STUDENT EDITION •

New York Times Bestselling Author

LEE STROBEL

with Jane Vogel

ZONDERVAN®

For Abigail, Penelope,
Brighton, and Oliver.
God's gifts of grace

ZONDERVAN

The Case for Grace Student Edition
Copyright © 2015 by Lee Strobel

This title is also available as a Zondervan e-book.
Visit www.zondervan.com/ebooks.

Requests for information should be addressed to:
Zondervan, 3900 Sparks Dr. SE, Grand Rapids, Michigan 49546

ISBN: 978-0-310-73657-8

Cover design: Deborah Washburn
Cover photography or illustration: Shutterstock
Interior design: Todd Sprague

Printed in the United States of America

15 16 17 18 19 20 21 /DCI/ 20 19 18 17 16 15 14 13 12 11 10 9 8 7 6 5 4 3 2 1

Therefore, if anyone is in Christ, the new creation has come: The old has gone, the new is here!

2 CORINTHIANS 5:17

CONTENTS

My Search for Grace

My dad was leaning back in his leather recliner. He looked back and forth between the TV and me, as if he couldn't be bothered to give me his full attention. He lectured and scolded and shouted, but his eyes never met mine.

It was the evening before my high school graduation, and my dad had caught me lying to him—big-time.

Finally he shifted to look straight at me. His eyes were angry slits behind his glasses. He held up his hand as he pounded each and every word: "I don't have enough love for you to fill my little finger."

He waited. He was probably expecting me to fight back, to defend myself, to blubber or apologize or give in— at least to react in some way. But all I could do was glare at him. Then after a few tense moments, he sighed, leaned back in his chair, and went back to watching TV.

That's when I turned my back on my father and walked out the door.

I didn't need him. I was driven and ambitious—I would slice my way through the world without his help. After all, I was about to make good money at a summer job. I'd be a reporter for a newspaper in the small town of Woodstock, Illinois, and I'd be living on my own.

A plan shaped in my mind as I slammed the back door and headed for the train station. I would ask the newspaper to keep me on after the summer. Lots of reporters had succeeded without college, so why not me? Soon I'd make a name for myself. I'd impress the editors at the Chicago papers and eventually break into the big city. I'd ask my girlfriend to move in with me. I was determined to make it on my own—and never to go back home.

Someday, there would be payback. The day would come when my father would unfold the *Chicago Tribune* and his eye would catch my byline on a front-page exclusive. That would show him.

I was on a mission—and it was fueled by rage. But there was one thing I didn't understand. What I didn't realize was that I was actually beginning a far different quest than what I had supposed. It was a journey that would someday reshape my life in ways I never could have imagined.

That day I started a lifelong search for grace.

CHAPTER ONE

The Mistake

it wasn't until my mother was dying that she confirmed what years of therapy had only suggested to me. I was a mistake, at least in the eyes of my father.

My parents started with three children—first a girl, then two boys—and my dad threw himself into fatherhood. He coached his sons in Little League, led a Cub Scout troop, went on family vacations, and attended gymnastics meets and graduations.

Then after a big gap came the unexpected news that my mother was pregnant with me.

"Your dad was ... well, let's just say he was surprised," my mom told me. We had never discussed this topic before. But as long as she was telling me about our family's history, I wanted some answers.

"Surprised how?"

She paused. "Not in a good way," she said, her eyes empathetic.

"He was—what? Angry?"

"I don't want to say angry. Frustrated, yes. Upset by the circumstances. This just wasn't in his plans. And then I talked him into having another baby so you'd have a playmate." That would be my younger sister.

This made sense to me. I had told my therapist about my relationship with my father. My therapist had guessed that my unexpected arrival had messed up my dad's plans for his future.

Maybe my dad felt that he had earned a break after raising three kids. He was doing well financially. I'm sure he wanted to travel and enjoy more freedom. What my mother said made sense.

Our family lived in an upper-middle-class neighborhood northwest of Chicago. My dad worked hard to build his business. He provided everything we needed—and more—materially. He was a faithful husband. He had a good reputation. He was loyal to his friends.

Still, my relationship with him was always frosty. Maybe I needed more affirmation than the other kids; I don't know. But by the time I came along, there would be no Cub Scouts, no cheering at my Little League games, no watching my speech tournaments or attending my graduations. I can't think of a single in-depth conversation we ever had. I never heard the words I needed most.

I learned that the only way to get his attention was through achievement. So I worked for good grades. I was elected president of my school. I served as editor of the school newspaper. I even wrote a column for the community paper. But I don't remember any words of affection coming from my dad. Not one.

My parents were members of a Lutheran church. My dad was a lawyer, and he gave the church free legal advice. But he was generally on the golf course on Sunday mornings.

I remember one time when I was a kid when the whole family went to church together. After the service, my dad drove everyone home—but he forgot to bring me. I can still remember how scared I was.

The Case for Grace

It was an accidental mistake, of course. But it was hard for me not to see it as a picture of our relationship.

FATHERS AND FAITH

Once when I was about twelve years old, my dad and I clashed over something. I felt guilty and ashamed afterward. I promised myself to try to behave better. I would be more obedient. Somehow I would make myself more acceptable to my dad. I don't remember what caused our fight that evening, but what happened next is still vivid in my mind.

I dreamed I was making a sandwich in the kitchen. Suddenly a glowing angel appeared! He started telling me about how wonderful heaven is. I listened for a while, then I said matter-of-factly, "I'm going there," meaning, of course, at the end of my life.

The angel's reply stunned me. "How do you know?"

How do I know? What kind of question is that? "Well, uh, I've tried to be a good kid," I stammered. "I've tried to do what my parents say. I've tried to behave. I've been to church."

Said the angel: "That doesn't matter."

Now I was staggered. How could it *not* matter? What else could I do? I didn't know what to say.

The angel let me stew for a few moments. Then he said, "Someday, you'll understand." Then he was gone — and I woke up in a sweat. It's the only dream I remember from my childhood. Now and then throughout the years it would come to mind, but I would always shake it off. It was just a dream.

As I got older, I found myself getting more confused about spiritual matters. When I became a teenager, my parents insisted that I attend confirmation classes at the church. (That's what kids in my church had to do to become full members of the church.) "But I'm not sure I even believe that stuff," I told my dad. His response was stern: "Go. You can ask questions there."

The classes were all about memorizing the Lutheran catechism; questions were not particularly welcome. I actually ended up with more doubts than when I started. I stuck it out because when I was finally confirmed, I'd be allowed to decide for myself whether to keep going to church — and I knew what the answer would be.

Back then I had no idea that a young person's relationship with his father can make a big difference in his attitude toward God. I didn't know that many well-known atheists throughout history had felt abandoned or deeply disappointed with their dads. I didn't know that problems with your father can make you less likely to want to know a heavenly Father.[1]

When I was older, I became friends with Josh McDowell. His father was a violent alcoholic. "I grew up believing fathers hurt," Josh said. "People would tell me there's a heavenly Father who loves you. That didn't bring joy. It brought pain because I couldn't tell the difference between a heavenly Father and an earthly father." Josh became what he called an "ornery agnostic." It took a long time for him to be convinced that Christianity is true.[2]

For me growing up, I just knew that I had doubts. My teachers insisted that science shows there is no God. I became more and more skeptical about Christianity. Still, something was missing — in my family and in my soul — that created a gnawing need I couldn't even describe at the time.

Even after I became a Christian, I felt an unnamed longing. Then one day I realized what I was missing. I was still looking for grace.

One day I was driving down Northwest Highway in Palatine, Illinois. I can still remember exactly where I was. I heard something on the radio that flooded my eyes with tears. I didn't catch it all, but it was about fathers and faith and God and hope. The speaker was about the same age I was. But my childhood was great compared to hers. I could hardly believe how much horror and brutality she had suffered in her life. Still, I felt an instant connection, a bridge between us.

I had to track her down. I had to sit down and hear her story, one-on-one. I had to ask her my questions. Somehow I knew she held a piece to the puzzle of grace.

The Case for Grace

CHAPTER TWO

The Orphan

Have you ever felt unwanted, like you didn't belong? If you have, then you can relate—at least a little—to Stephanie Fast.

Stephanie has never known her father. She suspects he was an American soldier—possibly an officer—who fought in the Korean conflict that started in 1950. There's even a chance he's still alive somewhere. There's no way to tell.

I managed to track down Stephanie, the woman I heard on the radio. I flew from Denver to her home in the Pacific Northwest to meet her. I was eager to hear her story.[3]

Stephanie was born in Korea—she's not sure just where. It might have been the region called Pusan; people have told her that her accent sounds like the people there. She's not sure exactly *when* she was born either, just that it was sometime around the end of the Korean War, when

American troops and the South Korean army were fighting against North Korean and Chinese troops.

Stephanie's earliest memory is of a Korean harvest festival when she was about three or four. Relatives from all over had come back to their hometown. They decorated the graves of relatives who had died. They danced and played games and ate sweets. Stephanie had a beautiful silk dress just for the occasion.

But late one night she heard some of her relatives arguing with her mother.

"We've found you a good husband," an uncle was telling Stephanie's mother. "It's a chance for you to have a better future. But he only wants you — not the child."

The child. That's me, Stephanie realized.

Even at that early age, she knew she looked different from other children. Her hair and skin color were lighter. She had wild, curly hair instead of the straight, shiny hair her cousins had. And she had a crease in her eyelids that most Koreans didn't have. (Nowadays, a lot of Korean women have surgery to get that eyelid crease. It's considered beautiful today. But back then, it was just one more sign that Stephanie wasn't pure Korean.) Biracial children were a reminder of an ugly war. And no one wanted that reminder.

"My mother had a choice to make," Stephanie told me as she recalled that night. "For her, the choice was, 'Do I want a future? If I do, then I can't have this child with me.' There was a lot of arguing and shame and guilt. I remember my mom crying and holding me all night."

At some point, Stephanie's mother made her decision. She would send her daughter away. Within a few days, Stephanie was at the train station with a lunch and a couple extra sets of clothing. Her mother got her settled on board and put Stephanie's things on a shelf above the seat. She got on her knees and told Stephanie, "Don't be afraid. Get off the train when everyone else does. Your uncle will meet you when you get off."

Then she left.

The Case for Grace

As Stephanie told me this story, I tried to imagine a three- or four-year-old taking a train trip all by herself. "What happened when you eventually got off the train?" I asked.

For a moment, Stephanie didn't answer. She slowly shook her head.

"No one came for me."

BASTARD

Here was a child not much older than a toddler, alone in a frightening and dangerous place among people who were likely to reject her—a world without grace.

At first, Stephanie wasn't scared. She waited for her uncle. But eventually night fell, and the trains stopped running. The stationmaster told Stephanie to leave. When she told him she couldn't— that she was waiting for her uncle—he spat out the word *tuigi*.

If you've ever read *Harry Potter*, you know that Malfoy calls Hermione a *mudblood*. That's the kind of word *tuigi* (pronounced "teegee") is. It literally means something like *child of a foreign devil*. People use it to imply that a biracial person isn't as good as a "pureblood" person. People say it with hate, the way a racist in the United States would use the N-word.

Remembering the first time someone called her *tuigi*, Stephanie mused, "It's odd—I'm sure my mom must have given me a name, but I can't remember it. It was like that day I became *tuigi*— garbage, bastard. That was what people called me."

After the stationmaster chased her away, Stephanie found a cart and clambered into it. She gathered some straw around her and ate the food her mother had sent with her. She tried to go to sleep, but she couldn't. All around her were scary sounds: barking dogs, strange noises, rustling on the streets. She was frightened. But she trusted her mom, and so she hung on to the thought that her uncle would come for her.

When Stephanie got to this point in her story, I had a question I wanted to ask. But I wasn't quite sure how to say it. I hesitated.

Finally, I asked, "Today as you look back, do you think there ever really was an uncle?"

She didn't flinch. "Honestly, I have no idea. It could be that she really was sending me to someone, but I made a mistake and got off at the wrong station. But in those days in Korea, it wasn't uncommon for mothers to abandon their children, especially if they were biracial. They would leave the children in train stations or other public areas."

"So, to this day, you don't really know whether your mother was really sending you to your uncle or if she was abandoning you?"

Stephanie looked down. "No, I don't," she said. Her eyes met mine again. "But I want to think the best of her. I have to, don't you see? I guess every orphan thinks of her mother as a princess. Still, she was under a lot of pressure; there's no question about that. Her whole future depended on it."

"I understand," I said. All of us, it seems, want to believe our parents have the best intentions.

BUGS AND RODENTS

Stephanie was basically on her own for two or three years. In the cities, charitable organizations were starting to rescue biracial children, but Stephanie was always in the mountainsides and villages.

"The first few weeks," Stephanie told me, "I cried for my mommy. I was always trying to find my way back to her. Maybe she would be over the next hill; maybe she would be around the next corner. If I saw a village from the distance, I would think, *Oh, that's my village*, and I would run into it.

"But it was never my village."

She quickly learned what it took to survive. She saw a group of homeless children crawl on their bellies into the fields to get some melons. She thought, *I could do that.* So every night, she would wait for the watchman of the field to fall asleep so she could steal from the farms and fields. As long as she didn't get caught, she could eat.

When she couldn't steal food, Stephanie caught grasshoppers and locusts. The rice fields were full of them. When she caught one, she'd poke a rice straw through its head. The next bug went on the straw, and the next, until she had a whole string of them. She'd tie the string of insects to her belt. By the end of the day, they were pretty much dried, and she'd eat them.

Sometimes she killed field mice. They would come out of the same hole at the same time every day. Stephanie learned to be really, really patient. When a mouse stuck out its head, she would grab it before it could go back down the hole. She ate everything — the skin, the ears, the tail.

Then winter came.

It was bitter cold, and Stephanie had nowhere to go and no food to eat. That first winter, she found a foxhole to live in. She gathered whatever straw she could find from the rice fields and brought it in to make a little den. She would go into the village when everybody was sleeping and steal what she could. Everything was a treasure. A tin can became her drinking can and boiling pot. She found nails and put them on the railroad tracks so the trains would run over and flatten them — they became utensils. She used one to gut the mice she caught.

Every once in a while, a kind woman would leave her kitchen door open, and Stephanie would curl up on the dirt floor by the stove and stay warm. But kindness was rare. Children picked on her because she was biracial, and farmers hated her because she was stealing from them. To everyone, she was a dirty *tuigi*. And when you're a little child and hear people call you that day after day, you begin to believe it about yourself. Stephanie believed anyone could do whatever they wanted to her because she was worthless. She was dirty. She had no name. She had no identity. She had no family. She had no future and no hope. Over time, she began to hate herself.

DOWN THE WELL

One day, Stephanie got caught stealing from a farm. The farmer seized her and dragged her to an abandoned well. Furiously, he lifted Stephanie up and heaved her into the well.

Stephanie panicked as she hit the water. She didn't know how to swim. As she thrashed and splashed in the dark, she hit a rock jutting out of the wall of the well just below water level. Clinging to the rough, slippery stone, she was able to keep part of her body above water. She screamed and screamed for help, but her voice just echoed back to her. No one came to help.

I'm going to die, she thought. And then, *Yeah, if I just let go, I can die. Maybe that would be okay.*

But she hung on. Hours passed before someone called down the well. "Little girl, little girl, are you down there?"

"Yes," Stephanie yelled back. "I'm here!"

She heard the *clang, clang, clang* of metal hitting rocks. Something hit her. Grabbing it, Stephanie realized it was a bucket on a rope. She hung on with all the strength she had left. Slowly, the person above pulled her from the well. Her savior—a grandmotherly old woman—half carried, half dragged Stephanie to a barn. There she covered Stephanie with straw to get her warm. Then she brought Stephanie some food.

The old woman told Stephanie, "These people, they will hurt you. But you must live. It's very, very important that you live."

Remembering those words now, Stephanie says, "As an adult looking back, I believe those words were prophetic. But as a little girl, I thought she must be telling me this because she knew my mommy. I thought she was suggesting that if I got up in the morning, left the village, and went over the next mountaintop, my mommy would be there."

But her mother never was.

THE WATERWHEEL

That wasn't the only time Stephanie heard those prophetic words. Once again, she was stealing food — and she got caught.

"Got you, *tuigi*!" A farmer grabbed her by the neck. "We've got to get rid of her," he said to the other farmers who had come to witness the commotion.

"Yeah, she's nothing but trouble. Let's tie her to the water-wheel!" another responded.

They grabbed Stephanie by her feet and shoulders and hauled her to the waterwheel on the canal. They tied her, face up, to the wheel. Stephanie screamed as she felt her legs being stretched, and then she choked as the turning wheel carried her under water. Pebbles and sand filled her mouth and nose as she was scraped along the riverbed. She spat it out, screaming and cursing, when the wheel brought her back up above the water. Then, suddenly, the waterwheel stopped.

"I felt a hand, and I heard a man's voice saying, 'Everything's okay. I'm going to take you off the waterwheel. Don't fight me,'" Stephanie recalls. "He took me off the waterwheel and set me on the ground. My eyes were so swollen I could hardly see him, but I do remember that he was wearing white. A lot of grandfathers in Korea wore white outfits back then. He took a handkerchief and cleaned me up as best as he could and gave me a drink of water.

"Then he said the same words as the woman who rescued me from the well: 'These people, they want to hurt you. You need to leave, but you must live, little girl. It's very important. Listen to me — you must live.'"

FROM GARBAGE HEAP TO HOPE

So Stephanie continued to struggle and survive. One day she wandered into Daejeon, one of the largest cities in South Korea.

An older boy approached her. "Hey, *tuigi*," he said, "You're new here in this town? Do you need a place to stay? You can come with me."

No one had ever invited Stephanie to stay with them before. She accepted eagerly and followed him to the river running through the city. The bank of the river had become a children's village. There were hundreds of orphans on both sides. Stephanie's new friend was a leader of a gang that oversaw everything. Stephanie's first few days there were wonderful. When members of the gang got food or blankets, they shared with her. They built bonfires and told folk stories, and when they went to sleep, Stephanie slept next to the boy and other children. For the first time since she'd left home, she was no longer alone.

But after a few days, the situation got bad. Stephanie became a sort of plaything for the older kids. One after another began sexually abusing her.

Stephanie was only seven.

"I figured that things like that must happen to everybody," Stephanie recalls. "I thought that's what I had to do to belong to a family."

After Stephanie had been living in this "family" for some time, a cholera epidemic swept through South Korea. Stephanie became very, very sick. Cholera causes extreme weight loss, high fevers, and delirium. Stephanie thought, *I've got to leave here. I'll go back into the country, where the air is better and I can get fresh food. Everything will be okay.*

She was walking through a dark alley when she saw a little girl in the gutter. Since people did not have flush toilets, everything ended up in that gutter. Stephanie was eager to get out of the city, but she just couldn't walk away from the other girl. But what could she do to help? She didn't have medicine, and she certainly didn't have a home she could offer to the sick girl. Both girls were hungry, so Stephanie did the only thing she knew to do: she stole some food.

And she got caught. So did the gutter girl. Their captors — four or five men — shoved them into a bombed-out building. Every street kid knew about this building. Lots of rats lived along the riverbank.

They moved in packs, and the kids were afraid of them. As long as the kids stayed together, the rats left them alone. But that building was the rats' territory.

Stephanie says, "When the men threw us into the building, I can recall picking that little girl up. I remember screaming. But that's the last thing I remember."

Her next memory is of opening her eyes and staring into blue eyes. Iris Eriksson was a nurse from Sweden. She worked with the Christian organization World Vision. Her job was to rescue babies from the street. At that time, children were being abandoned left and right. Korea was still trying to survive after the war, and if parents had more babies than they could feed, they just abandoned them. Iris was told to bring back the babies — not older kids like Stephanie. Babies were more likely to survive, more likely to get adopted, and less likely to have a lot of problems.

Here's the story Iris later told Stephanie. Iris found Stephanie on a garbage heap and realized Stephanie was more sick than alive. Of course, Iris felt sorry for her, but Stephanie was much too old for the clinic. Iris actually got up and was going to leave Stephanie there, but she said two things happened that changed her mind.

As she got up and was walking away, she said her legs felt really, really heavy. She didn't know why. As she was trying to figure it out, she heard a voice speaking Swedish. It only said two words: "She's mine." Iris was stunned, to say the least! Nobody was around her. She told Stephanie later, "I knew it was God — and I knew I had to answer him." So she did. She scooped Stephanie up and brought her to the clinic. Stephanie stayed there for a few weeks. Then, when she was healthy enough, Stephanie went to the World Vision orphanage in the city.

Remembering these events, Stephanie says, "Miss Eriksson — well, how can I put this? In a way, she was my savior before Jesus."

THE GIANTS IN THE ORPHANAGE

The orphanage became a house but hardly a home. The conditions were primitive: outdoor plumbing, mats for beds, and hundreds of children needing attention.

"I was one of the oldest ones," Stephanie recalls. "My job became caring for the babies, washing the diapers, hanging up the diapers, folding the diapers, changing the children, putting them on my back while I was working. I loved the babies."

Love — that was a word I hadn't heard during the story of Stephanie's journey. "Was this a new emotion for you, building relationships with them?" I asked her.

"Oh, yes. When I went into the baby section, they all had their arms out, wanting me to hold them. I felt loved. The workers didn't have enough time for all of them, so I would sing to them and hug them and carry them around. Then every once in a while, a baby would disappear."

"Disappear?"

"Yes, and when I would ask where the baby went, they would say, 'He went to America.'"

"Oh, so they were adopted."

"Well, that's the thing — I didn't know what adoption meant. I just knew that when they said a baby went to America, it was a good thing. So one day, the director said an American couple was coming to pick out a baby boy. I immediately started working to get them ready — brushing their hair, giving them baths, pinching their cheeks, putting them in the best rags we had available.

"The next day, the bell rang in the compound. A worker opened the door, and it was like a giant was coming in. Not only was he tall, he was massive. Back then in Korea, the only people with extra weight were rich, so I thought he must be the wealthiest person on the face of the earth. He stepped aside, and Mrs. Giant came in. She wasn't much smaller.

"They were speaking English and had an interpreter with them. The bassinets were lined up along the hallway, and I watched as the

The Case for Grace

man would pick up a baby and tuck it under his neck." Her face lit up at the memory.

"I was just overwhelmed by him; I don't think I had ever seen a man hold a baby like that. He brought the baby right up to his cheek, and he was kissing him and talking to him, and it was just ... well, an emotion began to rise in me. I saw him put that baby down and pick up another baby, and what I didn't realize was that I was inching closer to him. I was very curious.

"He put the second baby under his chin, and then I looked into his eyes — and he was crying. And my heart was starting to *pump pump pump pump pump* ... Something in me said, *This is good*. He put that baby down and did the same thing with a third one — and with the third one, he saw me out of the corner of his eye. He did the same, kissing and putting the baby down, and he turned around to look toward me — and I started backing up, backpedaling."

"When he looked at you, what was he seeing at that time?"

"Although I was almost nine years old and had been in the orphanage for about two years, I still had dirt on my body, especially my elbows and knees — it was ground into my skin. I had lice so bad that my head was actually white. I had worms so bad in my stomach that when they got hungry they'd crawl out of my throat. I had a lazy eye that sort of flopped around in its socket. I couldn't see very well at all, probably from malnutrition. My face was devoid of expression. I weighed a little less than thirty pounds. I was a scrawny thing. I had boils all over me and scars on my face.

"And yet still, he came over to where I was. He got down as low as he could, right down on his haunches, and looked straight into my eyes. He stretched out his enormous hand and he laid it on my face, just like this," she said, closing her eyes as she tenderly demonstrated with her own hand. "His hand covered my head; it felt so good and so right. And then he started stroking my face."

I sat spellbound as I listened to Stephanie's story. Here it was — the image of grace I had been seeking: a father bringing unconditional acceptance to a child who had absolutely nothing to offer, just herself in all of her vulnerability and scars and weaknesses.

My eyes moistened. *This* is the love of a dad. Maybe — *just maybe* — this is the love and grace of a Father.

SPITTING IN THE FACE OF HOPE

Then something incredible happened. "The hand on my face felt so good," Stephanie was telling me, "and inside I was saying, *Oh, keep that up! Don't let your hand go!* But nobody had ever reached out to me that way before, and I didn't know how to respond."

"What did you do?"

Her eyes widened, as if she were still astonished by her own actions. "I yanked his hand off my face," she said, "and I looked him in the eye — and I spit on him! Twice, I spit on him! And then I ran away and hid in a closet."

Spit on him? My mind was reeling. Grace was throwing open a window of opportunity for her — a chance for hope, security, and a future — and she deliberately slammed it shut.

"How?" I asked. "How could you possibly do that?"

Yet as she searched for a fuller explanation, my mind flooded with all the ways I had yanked God's hand off my face the many times he had reached out to me in my days of rebellion and skepticism.

There was the time as a child when a Sunday school teacher spoke glowingly about the love of God. I felt drawn toward faith — but uncomfortable with the emotions, so I pulled away. Or the time at a friend's wedding when the pastor spoke powerfully about building a marriage around Christ. I was intrigued, but quickly the busyness of my career doused my budding spiritual curiosity.

Or the time I cried out to the God I didn't believe in, desperate for him to heal my newborn daughter of the mysterious illness that was threatening her life. Suddenly — somehow, inexplicably — she recovered fully, but I promptly forgot about the prayer, chalking up the healing to a miracle of modern medicine, even though the doctors had no explanation for what happened. More than once, I had to admit, I had allowed the window of spiritual opportunity to slowly … slide … *shut.*

For Stephanie, in many ways, this could have been the end of her story. Still, incredibly, the man and woman at the orphanage were persistent. They continued to pursue her, despite her initial rejection of them. The next day, they came back.

"I was called into the director's office, and there was the foreign couple," Stephanie was telling me. "I was thinking, *I'm in real trouble now! I'm going to get punished for what I did to him. They're going to beat the tar out of me.* But the interpreter pointed to this man and this woman — these strangers, these foreigners, this enormous man with the huge heart who wept over children — and she said, 'They want to take you to their house.' "

What struck Stephanie was that this couple easily could have chosen a more likable child — perhaps the baby boy they had originally envisioned adopting. Nobody would have blamed them. Nobody would have given it a second thought. Nevertheless, David and Judy Merwin, newly arrived missionaries from the United States, unexpectedly declared on that day: *This is the child we want.*

"At the time, I didn't realize that I was being adopted," Stephanie said. "I thought I was going to become their servant. That's basically what happened in Korea: when a child got to be a certain age, he or she was sold as a servant to rich people."

A servant, yes, she could envision that. She could pay off their kindness; she could earn her room and board. Becoming a servant was the only way she could make any sense of her situation. A very understandable reaction.

FROM *TUIGI* TO PRINCESS

The Merwins had expected to adopt a boy and name him Stephen, so they gave their new little girl the name of Stephanie.

Their house in Korea, modest by Western standards, seemed huge to her.

"I had never seen a refrigerator, a flush toilet, or a bed before. I thought, *Wow, this will be a fun place to work!* They even had eggs, which only rich Koreans could afford. They cleaned me up, gave me antibiotics, and got me healthy. They kept feeding me, tucking me into bed, buying me new clothes, but never putting me to work."

"Did that confuse you?"

"Yes. I wondered why for several months, but I was afraid to ask. We'd go into a village, and everybody would treat me like I was something wonderful. I couldn't understand — I had been a *tuigi*, but now I was being treated like a princess.

"Then one day a girl said to me, 'You smell American.' I said, 'What do you mean?' She said, 'You smell like cheese.' Korean children always said foreigners smelled like cheese. I said, 'No, I'm not an American, but those Americans are really funny. They haven't put me to work yet. They're really treating me nice.'

"She looked at me with a surprised expression and said, 'Stephanie, don't you realize that you're their daughter?' That idea had never occurred to me. I said, 'No, I'm not their daughter!' And she said, 'Yes, you are! You ... are ... their ... daughter.'

"I was astonished! I turned and ran out of the room and up the hill toward my house, thinking to myself, *I'm their daughter, I'm their daughter, I'm their daughter! Oh, that's why I've been treated this way. That's why no one's beating me. That's why nobody's calling me a* tuigi. *I'm their daughter!*

"I ran into the house to my mom, who was sitting in a chair, and I declared in Korean, 'I'm your daughter!' She didn't speak Korean yet, but a worker said to my mom, 'She's saying she's your daughter.' With that, big tears began to run down my mommy's face. She nodded and said to me, 'Yes, Stephanie, you're my daughter!'"

"How did that make you feel?"

Stephanie had been speaking so candidly about her life, including unthinkable mistreatment and suffering, abandonment and

The Case for Grace

rejection, humiliation and pain. But now she was flustered. This time, words failed her.

"It was —" she began, then threw up her hands. "There are no words, Lee. There are simply no words."

Sometimes language cannot contain grace.

AND THEN, JESUS

"Your adoptive parents showed you so much love," I said. "Did that point you toward Jesus? How did you end up becoming a Christian?"

"We were at a beach in Korea, and my daddy asked me if I wanted to be baptized. I said, 'Sure, let's just do it in the ocean.' So my daddy baptized me."

"Did you really have faith at that point, or were you trying to please your parents?"

"I loved the Lord as much as I knew how, but I just had so much hurt inside. My problem was that I was scared to show people my pain. I thought if my mommy and daddy saw my pain, they would bring me back to the orphanage. If my teachers saw my pain, they would tell my parents. If my friends saw my pain, they'd tell my parents. I never wanted them to find out about my life as a street kid. I was afraid they'd reject me. That went on until I was about seventeen."

"What happened then?"

"We had moved to a small town in Indiana, where my father was a pastor, and I was doing everything to deny my Korean heritage. I was the only Asian in high school, and I wanted to be the perfect American girl. I was the homecoming queen and won the citizenship award, yet every night I'd go to bed scared to death I'd be discovered and lose my parents' love.

"Then the summer before my seventeenth birthday, I was sullen and irritable and withdrawn, and my mom gently confronted me. I stalked off to my bedroom, shut the door, and looked in the mirror.

I felt like I was still nothing but a *tuigi*, a piece of trash. I crawled under the covers of my bed.

"A little while later, my dad opened the door, and I heard him call softly, 'Stephanie?' He came in and sat next to my bed and said, 'Your mother and I want you to know that we love you very much, but you seem to have a hard time accepting that love. The time has come for us to release you to God.'

"Now, I was a pastor's daughter, so I knew the Bible, right? But my dad knew better. He said, 'Stephanie, can I share with you about Jesus?' I sort of rolled my eyes and said, 'Sure.' He told me to think about Jesus—he knows how I feel, and he is the only one who can help me. And then my daddy left me by myself.

"Until that moment, I only saw Jesus as the Son of God. I knew he had come down to earth, but that night, for the first time, it dawned on me: *He understands me.* He walked in my shoes! As a matter of fact, he was sort of a *tuigi*. You know? His daddy—his earthly father—wasn't his real daddy. He slept in the straw as a child. He was ridiculed and abused. They chased him and tried to kill him. *Oh, that's what Daddy means when he says Jesus understands me.*

"So after my dad left that night, I prayed—but my prayer was not a nice prayer. I said 'God, if you're what Mom and Dad say you are, then do something and do it right now!' And he did."

"What did he do?"

"I started crying. I hadn't cried in years; I hadn't been able to. When I was on the street, I learned that crying made me a target for bullies. But that night, something cold and hard broke inside of me—a barrier between me and God. He finally let me shed tears—and I couldn't stop them.

"I started wailing, and my mom and dad came into the room. They didn't say anything. I wouldn't let them snuggle with me, so my dad held my feet and my mom held my hands and they prayed silently to the Lord. And I had this supernatural intervention.

"Suddenly, it just came to me: Jesus knows me—*and he still loves me!* He knows all my shame, he knows all my guilt, he knows all my fears, he knows all my loneliness—yet he still loves me. And I've never been the same since.

"Before then when I would hear about God's love, I always felt it was love for everyone else. He couldn't love me, right? I was a mistake! He couldn't love me; I was born out of sin. He couldn't love me; I'm biracial. I thought you had to have some status in life to be loved. That was so ingrained in me that after I was adopted and my parents talked about the love of God, I still thought, *He can't love me! I was raped. He can't love me! I was abused. He can't love me! I have this awful anger inside. He can't love me! My daddy says I need to forgive, and I just don't want to.*

"But that night came the realization: *He. Loves. Me!* He loves me as I am. And that changed me, inside out. It took me many, many more years to let go of certain patterns in my life and to heal. I hated myself for so long. The fact that I could finally look in the mirror and love myself was nothing less than a miracle. It's God's grace.

"So these days, I have a phrase that I use. For me, I can honestly say there is no event in my life that I am better without. Why? Because everything in my life brought me to Jesus."

"I think I understand," I said. "But your story is so completely different from mine."

She took a sip from her cup of coffee. "Maybe we have more in common than you think," she said.

I wasn't sure what she meant. In an earlier conversation, in response to her questions about my background, I had mentioned the issues that prompted my exploration of grace, but I still didn't see the connection she was referring to.

"The Bible talks about orphans, but sometimes it uses the word *fatherless*," she said. "It sounds like your father protected and provided for you—believe me, that's good. You should be grateful for that, as I'm sure you are. But still, a person can be an orphan of the heart."

Orphan of the heart. I shuddered. Her words penetrated to my core.

"And that's where God can provide," she said. "That's where grace can come in. As the Bible says, 'God, ... you are the helper of the fatherless.'"[4]

Read it here

Find the Scripture about God as the helper of the fatherless in Psalm 10:14.

ADOPTED BY GOD

As I flew back to Denver the next day, I felt like I had looked into the eyes of grace. Once untrusting, uncertain, and anticipating the worst, today Stephanie is warm, gentle, and serenely confident. Such a remarkable transformation—first because of a father who sacrificed his dream of a son and reached out to her when she was a social untouchable, and then because of a Father who sacrificed his own Son in order to pour his healing love on her.

As Stephanie said, maybe my experience isn't so different from hers. What truly captivates me about grace is that God has not only erased the sins for which I deserved punishment, but he has also become my loving and compassionate Father, whose divine acceptance of me rushes in to fill a heart left parched by an earthly dad.

The truth is that God could have forgiven my past and given me assurance of heaven and yet kept me at arm's length. He could have made me a mere servant in his kingdom household—and even that would have been more than I merited. But his grace is far more outrageous than that. He has adopted me as his own child. It's just like the Bible says: "to all who did receive him, to those who believed in his name, he gave the right to become children of God."

Read it here

Find the verse about becoming a child of God in John 1:12.

The Case for Grace

Children of God—yes, I understood that God's grace invites us into his eternal family. But after hearing Stephanie's story, the grace of adoption struck me again. It registered deep inside of me.

I pictured Stephanie, running with joy toward home, declaring to herself, *I'm their daughter, I'm their daughter, I'm their daughter! Oh, that's why I've been treated this way. That's why no one's beating me. That's why nobody's calling me a* tuigi. *I'm their daughter!*

For me, I needed desperately to absorb this truth: I'm beyond forgiven. I'm more than a servant. I'm adopted by a Father whose love is perfect, whose acceptance is unconditional, whose affection is never ending and whose generosity is boundless. A Father who is *for* me ... forever.

Celebration was breaking out inside of me. *I'm his son, I'm his son, I'm his son! Oh, that's why I've been treated this way. I'm his son!*

CHAPTER THREE

The Addict

Do you ever feel as if your best isn't good enough? Scratch that. I know you do—because *everybody* feels like that sometimes. What would it take to be good enough?

Actually, that's the wrong question. But it can take a long time to realize that....

Jud's heart was racing. His body was soaked in sweat. He was dazed and disoriented as he slowly regained consciousness. He wasn't sure where he was. It took every ounce of his energy just to crawl out of the bed. There in the mirror, he barely recognized himself—sunken eyes, detached expression. After the amount of drugs he had taken, he was a little surprised that he was still alive.

That's when he did something that only another addict could understand. He mixed his remaining stash of drugs, drew a breath, and plunged the needle into his arm once again.

I might die, he realized. *And I'm okay with that.*

If anyone needed God's help, it was this seventeen-year-old Texan. After four years of descending into a hell of cocaine and methamphetamines, he was rushing headlong toward an early death.

So what becomes of an auto thief, a shoplifter, a slacker, a drug abuser who started injecting meth before he was old enough to drive? Well, there I was, sitting in his office inside a megachurch in Las Vegas.

Yes, now he's the pastor of a church. And because of his experiences, he has a generous attitude toward this town that's nicknamed "Sin City." A huge photograph of Las Vegas hangs on his office wall. Across the top in bold letters are the words *Grace City*. Along the bottom is Romans 5:20: "Where sin increased, grace increased all the more."

Sin and grace—I knew those themes were central to Jud Wilhite's story. But in our years as friends, he had never shared with me how he survived his near overdoses. I was anxious to hear what had happened, but I had traveled to Las Vegas for more than that.

What I wanted to hear about happened *after* Jud was adopted by grace into God's family. Soon he found that he had traded one addiction for another compulsion. This time, his "addiction" was performance and legalism. And it threatened to suffocate his faith.[5]

EXPERIMENTING WITH DRUGS

When Jud was twelve years old, he joined a group of students passing around a joint during lunch break at school. That was when he was introduced to drugs.

"It wasn't so much about getting high," he recalled. "It was more about wanting to fit in with the kids who were older than me.

"All addicts tell the same story," Jud said to me. "When it starts out, you go to parties and the drugs make you feel good. Like you're freer and can communicate better. But pretty soon, you don't even go to the party anymore. You're in a back room somewhere, doing the heaviest stuff you can find. You're on the path to jail, death, or insanity — one of those three. Unless you get clean, it's going to happen. And it didn't take me long to find my way to that back room."

Drugs were easy to get in Amarillo, Texas, where Jud grew up as a fourth child, with a big gap between him and the next oldest sibling — just like me. His dad was a former Army Master Sergeant who had fought at the Battle of the Bulge and later found success in owning a refrigeration business.

"Did your parents take you to church as a kid?" I asked.

"Yeah," he said. "I'd tell them I was going to the youth group, then I'd sneak out the back and walk around the alley, smoking cigarettes and waiting for church to be over. I'd meet them at the car afterward."

"Did they ever ask you about the youth group?"

"Oh, sure. They'd say, 'What did you learn about today?' I'd say, 'Jesus.' They'd say, 'What about him?' And I'd say, 'That he loves me.' I figured that was what they wanted to hear."

Pot and booze led to speed and cocaine. His life tumbled out of control. Police arrested him after he was caught shoplifting at a department store. When he was fourteen, he and some friends stole a neighbor's car late at night and took it on a joyride, with Jud behind the wheel — until they were busted by his dad.

For four years after he took his first drag of pot, everything was a blur. "I didn't know what it was like to face a week of life sober," he said.

He gestured at a guitar mounted on his wall, a memento from his days in a rock band. "It was like Johnny Cash said. After the first pill, every one he took was trying to recapture that first high — and it did nothing but drive him further from God and the people he loved the most. That was me."

"I CAN'T DO THIS ALONE"

After waking up from his overdose and then taking the remainder of his drugs — "I was daring death, in a way" — Jud drifted in and out of consciousness. At times, he vomited violently. He had hit bottom. For the first time in years, he wanted to be free—from drugs, from despair, from confusion.

"I was a fool," he told me. "I had been given every opportunity. I had a family that loved me. But I was completely deceived by sin. I looked around and realized that my life was a train wreck."

Over the next few weeks, he continued to smoke pot—it was as natural to him as breathing. But Jud also thought about his future. He was at a crossroad.

"I was on the edge of everything coming unraveled," he said. "I was so tired and worn out. I hated everything I had been doing. I hated the drugs, like so many addicts do. I felt like my time was running out. If I kept on the road I was on, sooner or later I'd hit a dead end. I was powerless to end the cycle of despair and guilt."

"So what did you do?"

"The only thing I *could* do—I cried out to God. I dropped to my knees in my bedroom and said: *God, help me! I'm messed up beyond belief. I need you!* It wasn't eloquent, but what else could I say? It was the truth."

"Then what happened?"

"Well, I didn't hear any voices or see any angels. But honestly, the sense I had in my soul was, **Welcome home**. I felt like I had arrived at the place where I belonged."

"And that was the beginning of your turnaround?"

"Absolutely. The next morning I had my drug paraphernalia laid out in my car. I was going sixty or seventy miles an hour down the freeway. I thought, *This is real now. What am I going to do?* I felt God giving me the courage to gather up all that stuff and throw it out the window. And that was it. I never went back."

"Did you go through withdrawal?"

"For days I was sweaty, clammy, cranky, irritable—yeah," he replied. "But I knew two things: I couldn't go back—that was simply not an option—and yet I couldn't go forward by myself. I needed a power that went beyond my own weak will. Every day, I

The Case for Grace

had to fight my desire for another high. It was a struggle; for a long time, it was tough."

"How did you manage to break through?"

"Over and over, I kept whispering a prayer: *I can't do this alone. God, help me. If you don't show up somewhere in my life, I'm through.*"

"And did he show up?"

Jud smiled, and then let out a chuckle. "Yeah, he did, but not in the way I ever expected."

"How?" I asked.

"Through the church."

RESCUED BY GRACE

At age seventeen, Jud walked across the parking lot and into the same church he'd been sneaking out of. For the first time, it was on his own terms. He wasn't there because he fully believed the Christian story—not yet, anyway. He just knew his life had been a mess and he couldn't overcome his addiction on his own.

He found his way to a back room where some young people gathered each week for a Bible study. Through this small community of Christians, he found Jesus.

"In some ways, they were the oddballs, the people who didn't fit in with the regular youth group," he said. "And frankly, that's what I was. A couple of them knew about my addiction, but most didn't. It didn't matter, though. They knew without knowing—you know what I mean? And they gave me a safe place."

"They showed you grace."

"Exactly. They didn't judge or condemn me. They didn't ask too many questions about my past or what I'd been involved in. They didn't sit me down and interrogate me. They gave me the freedom to tell them what I was comfortable telling them. They listened to me, they respected me, and they prayed for me—really, they talked me down off the ledge. They gave me the gift of time. They loved me like Jesus would."

Jud had discovered the Church.

Over the next six months, his appetite for God grew. He would come home from school, lock himself in his room, and read the Bible. He would hang out with members of the church group during the week. By January of his senior year, that prayer of desperation he had blurted out in his bedroom had truly been answered. He was fully, safely, securely Home.

More and more, the church became like a family to him. One day, he was walking down the hallway when he met the senior pastor going the opposite direction.

"Hey, Jud," he said. "Have you ever thought of becoming a pastor?" Just like that — out of nowhere.

Jud's first thought: *What's he been smoking?*

Still, a seed had been planted. The two of them met later, and the pastor told Jud that God had impressed on him that someday Jud would lead a church.

"How did you respond to that?" I asked.

"I prayed for two things. First, that God would let me use my experiences to help other people find the same kind of grace that had rescued me. And second, that he would allow me to do that through a local church, because God used the church to save my life."

At the time, Jud didn't foresee the biggest obstacle in his path.

Religion.

"I QUIT"

Fueled by gratitude for God's grace, Jud shifted into high gear as a Christian. He attended a Christian camp, met some musicians, and then played bass for a Christian rock band. ("What was the band called?" "Please, don't ask." "No, seriously — what was its name?" Pause. "Angelic Force." Awkward pause. "Okay, I'm sorry I asked.")

Later, he went to a Christian college. By his senior year, he attended classes during the week and preached at a small church outside of Dallas on Sundays. But somewhere along the way, the sincere desire to serve God morphed into the compulsion to prove over and over that he was good enough to deserve God's continuing love.

"For a long time, I had failed my family and God. So after I became a Christian, I got on a performance treadmill without realizing it," he explained. "I was putting pressure on myself to please God. I acted as if I had to be a super Christian. I wanted to make up for lost time and show that God was right to save me."

Jud fasted for days. He prayed endlessly. He served the homeless. He gave away everything he owned until all he had was a pair of jeans, a shirt, and shoes. People would talk about how mature he was as a Christian. But looking back, Jud now sees that he had the wrong motivation. And he wanted others to be as sacrificial as he was. When they weren't, he was critical of them. He became, in his own words, "a judgmental jerk."

He was missing the point of grace.

"I knew that I was saved by God's grace alone," Jud said, "but now I was trying to earn my keep. Jesus had paid my debt, but I felt like I needed to repay him. Still, no matter how much I did, it was never enough. In my mind, I kept falling short. I started to feel phony. Like I was only as good as my last performance—and my last performance wasn't very good."

I was nodding as he spoke, because I could relate to his story. After God's grace unshackled me from my atheism when I was in my twenties, I was full of energy to serve Jesus and tell others about him. I left my journalism career and took a sixty percent cut in pay to join the staff of a church. I was thrilled to spend the best hours of my day in ministry.

Like Jud, I knew that God had adopted me out of grace, not because of the good stuff I could do. But pretty soon, I found myself working feverishly to somehow show that he had made the right choice. I needed to prove that I was good enough for God after all.

> "Grace means there is nothing we can do to make God love us more ... and there is nothing we can do to make God love us less."
> — PHILIP YANCEY[6]

One night, I got a call from the church's senior pastor, Bill Hybels. "I heard a nasty rumor about you," he said.

I was taken aback. "Like what?"

"That you're working at the church sixty or seventy hours a week. That you're there late into the night and all day Sunday."

To be honest, I swelled with pride. *That's right,* I wanted to say. *I'm the hardest working member of the staff. Finally, it's time for some recognition and thanks—if not directly from God, then from my pastor.*

I said with some modesty: "Well, I am working hard, if that's what you mean."

Now his voice had an edge. "If you continue down that path, you're fired."

"What?"

"Something unhealthy is driving you. There's nothing you can do to make God love you any more than he already does. You need to believe that."

I told Jud my story, and now he was the one nodding. "That's the performance trap that snares so many Christians," he said. "Following all the rules perfectly to keep God happy. And condemning others because they aren't trying as hard as you. I got to the point where I was exhausted, frustrated, and miserable."

The performance trap:

Following all the rules perfectly to keep God happy, and then condemning others because they aren't trying as hard as you.

The Case for Grace

"So what did you do?"

Jud threw his hands up. "I quit!"

"You quit? How?"

"One day, I said, *God, I'm not good enough. I wasn't really a church guy before anyway. I'm a former addict, for goodness' sake. I can't do this Christian thing. I quit!*

"I figured I'd change my major at college and find some other career," Jud said. "I told God, *I still love you, but please don't ask any more of me.*"

"What changed your mind?" I asked.

"One day, I was reading 1 John 4:8–9, which says, 'Whoever does not love does not know God, because God is love. This is how God showed his love among us: He sent his one and only Son into the world that we might live through him.' That's when it registered for me: *it's all about God.* How I feel about God isn't as important as how God feels about me. It doesn't matter how good I try to be. What's important is how good God is. He never demanded that I become a super Christian in the first place. All he asked was that I love him in return. That was life changing for me.

"It all comes back to grace."

The insights that freed Jud were similar to the ones that led to my own recovery from spiritual workaholism. I came to realize that God didn't love me because I made myself valuable through service. I was valuable because God loved me. I could stop working like a slave to justify myself. I just needed to recognize — and celebrate — my adoption as God's child. My desire to love and serve God in a healthy way would flow from that.

Jud had the same experience. "After I rediscovered the beauty of grace, I began to relax in my faith," he said. "I started to enjoy God again instead of feeling like I had to prove something to him. Like where Jesus said, 'Come to me, all you who are weary and burdened, and I will give you rest.' The word *rest*, in Greek, means 'revive' or 'restore.' God offers to revive us from the inside out — and that's what he did for me.

Read it here

See what Jesus promised about reviving us in Matthew 11:28.

"I felt like I was free to laugh again. Free to be myself and to mess up. I stopped policing others and started loving them. I was free to be compassionate toward hurting people who didn't have their lives together or who might have lifestyles that were very different from mine. I stopped putting a lot of pressure on myself. I'm not perfect; I sin every day. But I've lowered my expectations of myself and others. And I've raised my expectations of God and his grace."

"As a pastor, has it changed the way you preach?" I asked.

"Pastors have to be careful. We encourage people to serve, to give, to be part of a small group, to read their Bibles, and so forth — all of which are fine as long as they're done out of gratitude to God. But if we subtly convey that this is how someone stays on God's good side, then we're opening the door to legalism.

"I've been there," he added. "And I'm not going back."

SIN CITY

Jud rarely has to convince people in Las Vegas that sin exists. They've seen it. Even though some people aren't sure there's a God, they believe in the devil.

"Our nickname [Sin City] came from sinners — drunkards, addicts, gamblers, failures, prostitutes, swindlers," Jud said. "In other words, people God loves."

A lot of people deal with so much guilt, shame, and brokenness that it can take years for them to allow God's grace to sink in. Jud tries to show people God's grace by following the example of Jesus.

"Jesus chose to spend time with the kinds of people that most religious leaders wouldn't be seen with. Cheats, thieves, prostitutes. Jesus doesn't delight in sin, but he liked being around these people. Maybe that's because they were well aware of their depravity, unlike many of the religious folks who masked it with hypocrisy.

"Think about the Samaritan woman who Jesus met at the well," Jud continued. "Of all the people in the world God could have made an appointment with — the politicians, the celebrities, the military conquerors — he decides to meet with this woman. She's not even fully Jewish. She's been divorced five times. And she's currently living with a guy."

Maybe you know the story. Jesus said to the woman, "Give me a drink." Offering a drink in those days was an act of friendship. So what Jesus was basically saying was, "Will you be my friend?"

"To me," Jud told me, "this says God loves broken people — and he loves to fix them. Look at her: she was transformed. So when I deal with people, I want to have Jesus' attitude."

"Nobody really knows the motivation in the heart of another person," Jud continued. "We can easily misread them based on how they look or dress. So why not give people the benefit of the doubt? If I have a choice of being harsh or gracious, I choose to be gracious — because that's the way Jesus has been with me."

"Sort of like the saying, 'Hate the sin, love the sinner,'" I said. "Do you think that's really possible?"

"Unfortunately, a lot of Christians hate the sin *and* the sinner. And it has given churches a bad reputation."

When I was a spiritual seeker investigating whether Christianity made sense, I needed time on my journey to Jesus. Nearly two years elapsed between the moment I walked into a church in suburban Chicago and when I received Jesus as my forgiver and leader. Along the way, I also needed to be confronted periodically by the Bible's hard teachings on sin, confession, repentance, judgment — and, yes, even on hell.

"Jesus modeled grace, but he also embodied truth," I said to Jud. "Are you shying away from the more challenging truths of the Bible in order to keep people coming back to your church?"

He chuckled. "Just this last weekend, I did a message on sexual purity. I told the congregation, 'Look, if you're dealing with sexual sin in your life, you need to run from it — but don't run away from God.' I didn't water down what the Bible teaches, but I also allowed room for people to process it. I said, 'If you're just starting a spiritual journey, you need to know that God loves you even in the midst of your sin.' I want to spell out biblical truth in a way that's accurate but also gracious and encouraging.

"You see, we want people to go on a journey, but we don't want them to just wander around aimlessly, without direction. We want to guide them with God's Word. For us, there's always a destination in mind, and that's the Cross. That's where we want to see them end up, receiving forgiveness and hope through Jesus' atoning death."

ADDICTED TO GRACE

Jud glanced at his poster of the nighttime Las Vegas Strip under the words *Grace City*. He gathered his thoughts and then offered a story about a woman who had been attending his church for a while.

"I'll call her Sadie," he said. "She was a dancer in the adult entertainment world. Basically, she was a stripper. Something started to draw her to our church. She would dance all night, finishing in the early morning hours on Sunday, and then come over for the early service.

"At first, she sat in the back of the balcony. Over time, she worked her way closer to the platform. Eventually, she was sitting in the front row. She soaked in everything. She heard about grace and truth. She examined her life. She felt the Spirit working in her. She counted the cost. Then one Sunday, she came up to me after a service and said she wanted to become a Christian.

"She told me her whole unvarnished story. When she finished, I said, 'If you make this decision to follow Jesus, what will it mean for you?' And she didn't flinch. She said, 'It's going to affect my career; it's going to affect my income; it's going to change my whole life.' I said, 'Well, what are you waiting for?' And her voice was firm; she said, 'I'm ready.'

"So she began to pray — not a tidy, fill-in-the-blank kind of prayer, but a raw confession, followed by sincere repentance and sort of a delightful childlike acceptance of God's gift of grace.

"When she said, 'Amen,' we opened our eyes. Her mascara was a mess; there were tears spilling down her cheeks. She reached out to give me a hug, and all she could say was, 'Thank you, thank you, thank you!'"

Jud beamed as he recalled the encounter. He was quiet for a moment, like he didn't know what to say to me next. "We baptized nearly two thousand people last year. Every one of them — like Sadie — has a story. And mostly, they're messy — sometimes *really* messy. But every single story matters to God."

He grinned. "I guess, in a way, I'm still an addict," he said. "I can't get enough of that."

THE RIGHT QUESTION

At the start of this chapter, I said the question "What would it take to be good enough?" was the wrong one. Maybe it's the right question if you're talking about who's going to make the team or who's going to win an audition. But when you're talking about Christianity, we're not the ones who have to be good enough. Jesus is. And believe me, he *is* good enough.

We don't have to try to become super Christians (and risk becoming judgmental jerks) to win God's love. Nothing you do can make him love you any more than he already does. And nothing you do can make him love you any less. That's grace.

CHAPTER FOUR

The Good Guy

i f you're reading this book, you're probably a pretty good person.

I mean, how many really *bad* people read Christian books? Even if you're reading this as an assignment, at least you're the kind of responsible person who actually does assignments.

So here's my question: Do you need grace? You've probably already figured out that the "right" answer is yes. But what I really mean is, do you *feel*—do you know deep down in your gut—that you need grace?

Usually, the stories we hear are from axe-murderers-turned-missionaries, strippers-turned-Sunday-School-teachers, or abortionists who now march against *Roe v. Wade.* Or drug addicts like Jud from chapter three, or desperate street kids like Stephanie from chapter two. It's pretty clear that people like that need to be saved; they need grace. Their stories can be really inspiring. But what about all the decent people living in basically decent situations? How do they even come to the point of recognizing their need for grace?

Of all the people I knew, I figured Craig Hazen would have answers.

"NICE GUYS DON'T NEED GOD"

Craig Hazen has always been a good guy. He was a teacher's favorite in high school because he liked to learn. When he walked into the library, he felt like he was on a treasure hunt.

Craig was a science geek. He worked after school as an assistant to a doctor. He was planning a career in medical research. Sure, he was a prankster (once he started a donut fight so massive that it's now legendary at his old school), but he was clever enough to get away with it. The honor roll—that was no problem.

As for nice guys, they don't need God. At least that was Craig's opinion. As a teenager, he became an agnostic, figuring that science—not God—held the keys to understanding the big issues of life.

Still, there was that chemistry teacher, the one who kept putting posters about God on her classroom walls. She had an undeniable sense of peace that intrigued him. And there was the cute girl who invited him to church one night to hear a Christian speaker and a musician.

As he sat in the church that evening, Craig's analytical mind began to see this whole experience as a grand experiment. What if he were to go forward when the speaker invited people to give themselves to Christ? What would he have to lose? What might he gain? And how could a budding scientist resist the chance to find out? Who says you can't put God in a test tube?

Craig went forward, then he was ushered into a side room for counseling. "I thought, *Uh-oh, this is where the brainwashing takes place.* Before long, all the counselors were clustered around me, because I was peppering them with questions that nobody could answer."

"So you walked out that night unconvinced?"

"Pretty much. But I had started a journey. They began giving me books and tapes and following up with phone calls. I studied the issues for several months, and finally, doggone it (yes, he really said *doggone it*—I told you he was a wholesome guy), God sealed it. I became convinced Christianity is true.

"And then I began to understand why I had been attracted to the peace that I had seen in my chemistry teacher—the one who kept putting God posters on the walls. Even though I was a good kid, I was still a sinner, and I was feeling a sense of anxiety and alienation that I couldn't quite put my finger on. God began to deal with that in my life.

"In fact," he continued, "here's a funny thing about grace. A couple of years later, evangelists came to the college I was attending and brought some guys who had very dramatic testimonies. They stood on the cement planter in the quad and told about how they had been in the gutter and did all kinds of horrible things, yet the Lord found them and lifted them up. And I was thinking, *Man, I want to jump up there, too, but I want to give a different testimony.* You see, I *wasn't* in the gutter. I *wasn't* the dreg of society. I had great promise; everybody thought I was on the road to success. And guess what? I still desperately needed God!

"Here's what I came to understand: having good table manners, getting A's in school, saying please and thank you, and being nice to people—that's all pretty trivial stuff. Actually, I was in rebellion against a holy God so powerful that he could speak billions of galaxies into existence. Now, that's *huge*! I was ignoring him. I was turning my back on him. And my sins—my pride, my smugness, my selfishness, and all of my secret deceit and illicit desires—had created an enormous gap between us, and it was fostering that sense of alienation and anxiety in me.

"That's what sin does. God is perfect. He is holy. He is pure. And I certainly wasn't, neither in thought nor deed. The Bible stresses that nobody is truly good—Romans 3:23 says, 'for all have sinned and fall short of the glory of God.' Over time, I came to realize that the plain language of that verse means exactly what it says: 'all have sinned,' and that includes me.

"I needed forgiveness, and I found grace through Jesus."

BEYOND MERCY TO GRACE

"I've been looking into Islam," I said, "and even though Muslims see Allah as being stern and aloof, the Koran certainly talks about mercy."

"Islam does talk about mercy, but the grace that the Bible talks about goes much further than that," Craig said. "You see, in Christianity, God isn't just saying, 'I'm not going to punish you for what you've done.' That would be merciful. But he takes a dramatic next step by giving us something glorious — complete forgiveness and eternal life as a pure gift.

"It's like parents who catch their kids doing something wrong, and they don't just let them off the hook but give them ice cream as well, because they love them so much," he said, flashing a smile. "That's what grace is — an amazing gift that we don't deserve and can't earn or even contribute to. God gives it freely to those willing to receive it. We can't repay him for it. We can't take any credit for it, but God offers it because he made us in his image and wants to have a relationship with us for eternity. That's the Good News of the gospel. But to fully grasp it, we have to understand the bad news, as well."

"By bad news, you mean sin," I said.

"That's right. You can't really have a strong sense of grace unless you really understand sin."

"And that," I said, "is a problem these days — many people have lost the concept of sin."

"Absolutely. Take the Mormons, for instance. They don't think there's a very big gap between human beings and God. In fact, they think humans and God are the same species — like, if you take enough vitamins and so on, then you can become a god," Craig said. "But in Christianity, the gap that our sin creates between us and God is simply too big to cross by yourself. Trying to cross it is like jumping off the pier in California and trying to leap to Hawaii.

"The first time, you don't get very far, so you train harder and harder," he continued. "You work with the best long jumpers in the world, you buy new athletic shoes, you lift weights, and you eat your spinach — and the next time, you manage to jump twelve inches farther. Good for you! But the gap is still so huge. To get across a divide that wide takes an almighty and all-loving being to provide a bridge — which is what God does through the cross of Christ."

"What do you say to people who don't think they need grace? How do you answer someone who says, 'I'm a nice person. I like God. I may not be religious, but I'm very spiritual'?"

Craig thought for a moment. "There's a technique that evangelist Ray Comfort uses. He quizzes people on whether they've really lived according to the Ten Commandments. He asks, 'Have you ever lied?' And the person says, 'Hmmm, yeah.' Comfort says, 'Then you're a liar. Have you ever stolen anything?' They say, 'Well, yes.' And he says, 'Then you're a thief.' He goes through a list of sins and gets people to admit they've been wicked in many ways, but they just haven't recognized it.

"That's one approach to helping people see their own sinfulness so they'll also understand their need for forgiveness and grace. It's hard to think seriously about grace until you understand that you've failed morally and will someday stand accountable before a holy God."

He shrugged. "Granted, Comfort's approach is a little bit in-your-face," he said. "But sometimes we have to find ways to sort of shake people."

I pointed to the Bible on the table between us. "Which teaching of Jesus best illustrates grace for you?"

Craig was quick to respond. "It's got to be the story of the Prodigal Son. It's over the top! It really does show how we're not just talking about mercy; we're talking about a God who's singularly focused on having a love relationship with us and is willing to do just about anything for that.

Read it here

Find the story of the Prodigal Son in Luke 15:11–22.

"In this parable, the son takes his inheritance and says, 'I'm going my own way.' The father probably took a deep breath and said, 'Oh, I hope one day he comes back!' And after a disastrous life, the son *does* come back. The father sees him coming and, without a moment of hesitation, runs to him with presents and throws him a party. Now that's a story of grace!"

OF FLIES AND FLOUR MILLS

The story of God's grace has been the subject of poetry, paintings, and literature—but is it the stuff of logic? Ultimately, does it make sense? I asked Craig for his opinion, and I got a logical response.

"From one perspective, no. Grace is too over-the-top to be logical," he said. "And yet from another angle, it does make good sense. Psychologists will tell you that for children to thrive, unconditional love has to be part of the package. God wants us, his children, to thrive. If the system were set up so that you had to earn your way to God, you wouldn't know how much you needed to do or whether you'd made it or not, and you would live in a terrible state of anxiety."

An illustration I had heard years earlier popped into my mind. "It would be like a salesman being told by his boss that he must meet his quota or be fired—but then never letting him know what the quota was," I said.

"Exactly. For example, Islam is based on earning your way to God by doing more good deeds than bad ones. Officially, Muslims can't know if they've pleased Allah, so they have to do everything they can to pile up the good deeds."

"So what happens?" I asked.

The Case for Grace

"Let me give you an example from an influential Muslim leader concerning the month of Ramadan, when Muslims are to fast. He was thinking of different things that might interrupt his fast. He was very concerned about this, because he wanted his good deeds to outweigh his bad deeds, so at least he would have a shot of making it to paradise.

"Suppose a man is sitting in a chair during Ramadan and falls asleep. His head cocks back, his mouth falls open. A fly comes through an open window and darts into his mouth and out again. Has his fast been ruined? The leader analyzes this situation and similar ones for several pages — like, what if dust gets in your mouth? Well, could you have anticipated there would be dust in the air? Did you know that you would be driving on a dusty road? What kind of dust was it? Was it dust from the road or from a flour mill? All of these appear to be very important considerations.

"He goes on, page after page, and by the end, you sort of collapse in exhaustion — all the things you've got to track in order to make sure that day's fast gets fully credited so you've got a possibility of going to paradise. Now do all Muslims live that way? No, of course not. And yet if they really take the Koran's teachings seriously, they're pushed toward this kind of mind-set."

Craig threw up his hands and sat back in his chair. "Oh, my goodness, give me grace!" he declared. "Give me the father of the Prodigal Son! He is our only hope."

A FAITH THAT CAN BE TESTED

Craig's analysis of Islam led me to a related question. I've heard some astounding stories of people who have found grace through Christ, and their lives have been radically transformed as a result. In fact, I'm an example of that, as are several people I have interviewed for this book.

"And yet, there are Muslims, Hindus, and members of other religions who claim they've been fundamentally changed for the better because of their faith," I said. "So how does a transformed life count for the truth of Christianity — or doesn't it?"

"On the one hand," Craig replied, "I've seen examples of people who have been so personally revolutionized that I can only attribute it to the work of Christ. So, yes, I believe that a Christian's testimony about the power of God in their life can be persuasive, though it needs to be combined with other evidence to really make the case for Christianity.

"On the other hand, people in other religions also claim to have meaningful religious experiences. I remember teaching a class on world religions at the University of California at Santa Barbara, and we all drove to Los Angeles to tour religious sites. At the Krishna Temple, they invited us to observe their worship. They had tambourines and drums, and they were chanting and dancing. Afterward, one of my students seemed bothered. He said, 'I'm having trouble seeing the difference between what they do and what we do. It *felt* the same.'

"As I explained to this student, it's true that people in other religious movements can have wonderful experiences that make them feel spiritually uplifted. In fact, lots of things can give us what seems to be a 'spiritual high.' So we can't really go by just our feelings.

"Yes, you want to be transformed by your faith, but you also want to know that it's the real deal. So while grace sets apart Christianity, so does truth. Jesus was filled with grace *and* truth, and in Christianity, you can *know* the truth, not just through some sort of spiritual experience, but also through careful investigation.

"In other words, Christianity can be tested. And when you check it out — as I know that you did, Lee, when you were an atheist — you find that it's supported by philosophy, science, and history."

WANT TO KNOW MORE?

When I was an atheist, I investigated Christianity. (Honestly, in many ways, I was hoping it was wrong. But I became convinced that it is true. That's how I became a Christian.) Read the story of my investigation in *The Case for Christ Student Edition.*

My cell phone buzzed, signaling my need to end our conversation so I could drive to San Diego for another meeting. I packed up my gear and thanked Craig for his time as we stood to shake hands.

"Honestly," he said with that boyish smile, "there's nothing I enjoy discussing more than grace. It's an inexhaustible topic."

Over the next ninety minutes, as I drove through the snarled roadways of Southern California, signs of a diverse religious culture were everywhere. The woman in the hijab pushing a stroller down the sidewalk. The statue of Buddha in the window of a Vietnamese café. The driver wearing a yarmulke in car next to mine. The tidy Kingdom Halls of the Jehovah's Witnesses. The massive stone Mormon Temple, its spires reaching heavenward, that looms next to the freeway in San Diego. So many beliefs, each with their own demands and rules and requirements and expectations — to-do lists that never quite get completed.

And everywhere I drove, on top of Lutheran, Episcopal, Methodist, and Baptist churches, both traditional and modern, crosses rose toward the sky — not just a reminder of the unique message of freely offered grace, but so much more than that: a symbol of the unimaginable cost that was required to purchase it.

CHAPTER FIVE

The Executioner

A re there some people you don't want to see saved?

Nazi war criminals, maybe. That POW camp guard in *Unbroken,* the movie and book about Louis Zamperini's life. Comrade Duch of the Khmer Rouge.

But let me back up....

I had come a long way in piecing together the riddle of grace. Stephanie Fast reminded me how God's grace doesn't just forgive us, but it clears the way for us to be adopted into his very family for eternity. Jud Wilhite—snatched by God from the verge of self-destruction—cautioned against trying to prove we're worthy of grace even after we've received it as an unmerited gift. And Craig Hazen affirmed that even good guys need grace.

But what about the bad guys? The really, really evil people? Where does God draw the line? Surely there must be limits. If there were ever a case of grace going too far, where God shakes his head and turns his back, Christopher LaPel has seen it.

Christopher grew up in Phnom Penh, Cambodia. His father was a Buddhist high priest and spiritual advisor to Prince Norodom Sihanouk. Sometimes Christopher's father took Christopher to the palace, where he would play with the prince's children. One day, Christopher saw some of the royal craftsmen and asked them to make him a cross out of ivory.

Trivia

The *Guinness Book of World Records* later named Norodom Sihanouk as the modern royal who had held the most political positions.[7]

"A cross?" I asked Christopher when he told me this story. "Why would a Buddhist child ask for a cross?"

"I don't really know why. Maybe it was because I used to see one on a Catholic church. My siblings had Buddhist statues, but for some reason, I was fixated on getting a cross. To me, it represented power and purity. The craftsman made the cross, and I put it on a gold chain. It hung right here, under my shirt," he said, tapping his heart.

One day, Christopher was eating with his family. The Cambodian custom was to sit on the floor with food in the center. When Christopher reached to get something, the cross fell out of his shirt. Everyone looked. His dad was angry. He pulled Christopher toward him and said, "You shouldn't wear that cross! Remember, we are a Buddhist family."

He offered to make Christopher any Buddhist image he wanted, but Christopher didn't want anything else. He just moved the cross to hang down his back so it wouldn't fall out again.

When Christopher was nineteen, the communist Khmer Rouge took over Cambodia. They burst into the LaPel home with AK–47s and said, "You have to leave as soon as possible. Don't take anything. In three days, you will come back."

Christopher and his family joined a flood of residents who clogged the narrow roads, walking, running, some riding bicycles and motor scooters, carrying everything they could and wearing whatever valuable jewelry they had. Christopher wore his cross. There was mass confusion, chaos, and panic.

"Everyone was scared," Christopher recalled. "I was terrified. My dad said, 'Just do what they ask.' Three days turned into three weeks. Then we realized—we would never get back home."

So began their quest to avoid the massacres that would come to be known as the Killing Fields.

MYSTERY OF THE CROSS

Over the next 1,364 days, the Khmer Rouge, under the leader Pol Pot, was responsible for killing, starving, or working to death about two million Cambodians—one quarter of the Cambodian population. Accounting for the percentage of people destroyed, Pol Pot's communist regime was the most murderous in the modern age.

The goal was to destroy the social classes and create a society of farmers. "Teachers—dead. Former government workers—dead. Journalists—dead," Christopher said to me. "They wanted to get rid of anyone who was educated, so they would not be a threat. A friend of mine admitted to the Khmer Rouge that he was in college. He disappeared."

In fact, out of 11,000 university students at the time, only 450 survived. Just five percent of secondary students lived through the genocide. As for doctors, nine out of ten were killed.[8] Money was abolished, personal property confiscated, schools shuttered, courts closed, religious practices suppressed. Masses of people were driven into the rice paddies as slave laborers.[9]

In other words, it was an entire culture without grace.

"The Khmer Rouge would question us," Christopher said. "We had to be careful—one slip and we were dead. They would say, 'Who are you? Have you been to school?' They shoved a notebook in front of us. 'Here, write your name.'

"I wrote my name with my left hand, so it looked awkward. I said I was a farmer with just a couple years of school. They tested us: 'If you want to raise beans, what do you do?' In Phnom Penh, we would plant some corn and vegetables, so we knew a little. We were able to convince them we were farmers."

Christopher was separated from his family. He had to work in the fields to grow rice and build irrigation canals. He worked twelve to fourteen hours a day. At night in the summer, he worked by moonlight. Food was a watery soup plus any lizards he could catch. His weight dropped to ninety pounds; his hair was falling out from malnutrition. At night, the Khmer Rouge would call out names, and people would disappear from their huts, never to be seen again.

"At one point, I got very sick with a high fever," Christopher told me. "I missed three days of work. One night, a voice called out my name. It was the Khmer Rouge. They dragged me from my hut. That was it—I knew I would be killed. I was scared; I was trembling.

"They told me to sit on the floor, and they asked me why I hadn't been working. I told them I was sick but had no food or medicine. One said, 'What kind of sick are you?' I said, 'I have a high fever.' Someone said, 'Let's see how sick you are.'

"They began checking me. One put his hand on my head; another, on my shoulder. Then one opened my shirt—and that exposed the cross, hanging by a string. The light reflected off the ivory. There was silence, it seemed for a long time. Then there was a voice from somebody I couldn't see. He said, 'Well, this guy is really sick. We'll let him go.'"

I was inching toward the edge of my seat as Christopher told the story. "Thank God!" I said. "But why did they react that way to the cross?"

"I don't know why. They told me to go rest. The next day, they gave me Chinese medicine and rice soup and treated me very well. A few days later, I got better. I don't know what it was about that cross, but I believe it saved my life."

Still, staying alive got harder and harder. The brutality of the

The Case for Grace

Khmer Rouge was relentless. Christopher often heard people begging for their lives before they were executed.

He weighed his options and decided he had nothing to lose by running away. He escaped one night, navigating the jungle by moonlight. Eventually, he arrived at a refugee camp in Thailand. It had a name he didn't quite understand: Christian Outreach.

"I was so relieved, so happy to be there," he said. "I felt safe for the first time in so long. Then one day a woman shared with me about Jesus Christ. She talked about how he had died on the cross, and I thought, *The cross?* I said, 'Tell me the meaning of the cross. Why did he die?' She told me about how he died so I could be saved from my sins.

"At that moment, I remembered my ivory cross and how God had saved my life when I was sick. I prayed, 'Lord, I was supposed to die that night, but you spared me. I want to commit my life to serving you, no matter what you want me to do. My life is yours.'"

He went to feel the cross around his neck, but it was gone. Somewhere in the jungle, the string had broken. He grinned at the memory. "I had lost my cross," he said, "but I had found Jesus."

In the camp, Christopher met and fell in love with another refugee named Vanna, and they married. Eventually, they immigrated to the United States, where Vanna had a sister. Christopher graduated from a school fittingly named Hope International University and became a pastor of Golden West Christian Church in Los Angeles, California, located on a street called Liberty. Hope and Liberty — perfect!

Christopher never forgot Cambodia. He goes back and forth to his homeland to train and equip Christians. Today, more than two hundred churches can trace their origins back to his ministry.

THE HORROR OF S - 21

Other members of Christopher's family were not as fortunate. While he was still held captive in Cambodia, he got word that the

Khmer Rouge had worked his father and mother to death. His sister was killed. So was his brother.

"Then there was my cousin," he said. "She was a scientist who taught at a school ... She was arrested and taken to S–21."

The notorious S–21 was just outside of Phnom Penh. The Khmer Rouge used it as an interrogation, torture, and execution center. The "S" stood for *sala*, which means "hall," and the "21" was the code for *santebal*, or security police.[10]

Those living nearby only knew the facility as "the place where people go in but never come out."[11] Every prisoner was assumed guilty of treason when he or she entered. In fact, the traditional Cambodian term for prisoner literally means "guilty person."[12] A Khmer Rouge slogan was "Better to destroy ten innocent people than to let one enemy go free."[13]

The man in charge of S–21 was known simply as Comrade Duch (pronounced *doik*).[14] He was brutal, efficient, and surprisingly concerned about keeping records. With chilling precision, he documented every torture session, every forced confession, and every murder.

All prisoners were photographed when they arrived. On a list of eight teenagers and nine children, Duch wrote the order: "kill them all." On another order, he wrote, "use the hot method, even if it kills him." His notations for other prisoners included "take away for execution," "keep for interrogation," or "medical experiment."[15]

Sometimes the S–21 torturers would force confessions by hanging prisoners upside down, their heads in buckets of urine and feces. Other times, the guards used electric shocks, suffocation with a plastic bag, or beatings with electric cords. To save on bullets at executions, the executioners used knives, shovels, and hoes to slit throats, bash in heads, and break prisoners' necks. They killed babies by dropping them from balconies or swinging them by their legs and smashing their heads against trees.[16]

Four years after they had taken power, the Khmer Rouge was overthrown. Soldiers found fourteen bloated bodies, sticky pools of

The Case for Grace

blood, and torture instruments at S–21. Duch hadn't had time to destroy the records before he fled. As you can imagine, this did not please the leaders of the Khmer Rouge! But they didn't get a chance to discipline Duch. He disappeared and was presumed dead.

During the Khmer Rouge's reign of terror, more than 14,000 prisoners entered S–21. Only seven people are known to have survived. Christopher's cousin and her boyfriend were among those buried in shallow graves nearby.

"I weep when I think of what happened to her," Christopher said. "S–21 is now a genocide museum. There are hundreds of mug shots of prisoners on the walls."

He blinked away tears. "We found the picture of my cousin."

His body language was clear. He didn't want to say anything more about it.

A CHANGED LIFE

Fifteen years after the defeat of the Pol Pot regime, Christopher and a team from his congregation bought farmland and built a church in the Battambang Province in northwestern Cambodia. The following year, he led two weeks of leadership training for a hundred local Christians.

One of his key leaders invited a friend, Hang Pin, who was a teacher in a village not far away. Hang was a scrawny man; his most distinguishing physical characteristic was that his ears stuck out. He spoke Thai and some English and had taught for a while at the Foreign Languages Institute in Beijing, China.

Although he wasn't a Christian, Hang agreed to attend Christopher's training because he was suffering from depression and was looking for encouragement. Invaders had broken into his house. His wife, Rom, was bayoneted to death, and Hang was stabbed in the back—a traditional Khmer Rouge punishment for betrayal.[17] He recovered, sold everything he owned, and moved to teach at a college in the Svay Chek district.

"He was shy, quiet, very withdrawn, and discouraged. He sat in the back," Christopher recalled.

Christopher usually ended his sessions with an altar call, asking anyone who wanted to receive Christ's forgiveness to come forward. Most of the people in attendance were already followers of Jesus, so generally only a few responded. At the end of one class, Christopher was surprised to see that Hang had joined several others in stepping forward.

"I said to him, 'I'd like to pray for you. Do you have anything to say?' Hang said he had done a lot of bad things in his life," Christopher told me. "He said, 'I don't know if my brothers and sisters can forgive the sins I've committed.' He was sorry."

"Did you ask for any details?"

"No. I was more concerned about the present than the past. All I needed to know was whether he was repentant and if he understood that forgiveness is a gift of God's grace. And, yes, he did. I told him, 'God loves you. He can forgive you.' I prayed with him, and the next day, I baptized him in the Sangke River. Rarely have I seen such an immediate transformation in anyone."

"Really? How so?"

"His attitude, the way he acted—everything changed. Now he was sitting in the front row. He was dressed more neatly; he was excited; he would ask questions and interact with enthusiasm. He couldn't get enough teaching. He paid the most attention of all the students. He took notes and read the Bible eagerly. He couldn't wait to start a church in his village."

Before long, Hang received his certificate for completing the training. "I remember when we took our group picture," Christopher said. "He was standing right next to me in the front row. I put my hand on his shoulder."

Later, Christopher got the word that Hang had led his children to Christ and baptized them. After that, he planted a house church. Soon, there were fourteen families in the church. Hang stayed in contact with Christopher and went back for more leadership training.

Two years later, military violence forced Hang and the other villagers to leave the area. Hang ended up in Ban Ma Muang, a camp of 12,000 refugees inside Thailand. He began to serve with the American Refugee Committee, training health workers. He saved countless lives by helping stop a typhoid outbreak.[18]

When Cambodia became less dangerous, Hang returned and worked closely with World Vision, a Christian aid ministry, to provide health care to women and children.

Over time, Christopher and Hang lost track of each other. That is, until a phone call woke Christopher up one morning.

THE CALL THAT CHANGED EVERYTHING

The caller identified himself as a reporter for the Associated Press. "Could you help us identify one of your students?" he asked.

"One of my students?" Christopher replied. "Many people have come through my training."

The reporter described this individual — not very tall, skinny, his ears sticking out.

"Yes, I know him," Christopher said. "Hang Pin. He's one of our lay pastors."

"Well, he's hard-line Khmer Rouge," said the reporter.

Christopher's mouth dropped open. "What do you mean?"

"He was one of the top Khmer Rouge. He's a killer. He's a mass murderer. He was in charge of S–21. Hang Pin is Comrade Duch!"

Christopher's mind raced from his murdered cousin to the S–21 museum to baptizing Hang Pin. *Is this possible? How can this be?*

Slowly, the story emerged. Photojournalist Nic Dunlop had tracked down Duch in his village. Then Dunlop and investigative reporter Nate Thayer confronted Duch about his identity.[19]

At first, Duch was evasive. But quickly, he began admitting his past. "It is God's will you are here," Duch said to them. "Now my future is in God's hands. I have done very bad things in my life. Now it is time to bear the consequences of my actions."

Dunlop and Thayer showed Duch copies of the documents he

had signed to authorize executions. Even to a jaded foreign correspondent like Thayer, it seemed that Duch was genuinely sorry.

"I am so sorry. The people who died were good people," Duch said, tears in his eyes. "The first half of my life, I thought God was very bad, that only bad men prayed to God. My fault is that I didn't serve God. I served men; I served communism. I feel very sorry about the killings and the past. I wanted to be a good communist."

Now, he said, he had a new goal: "I want to tell everyone about the gospel."

Duch readily confessed to his crimes and said he would testify against other Khmer Rouge officials so that they, too, could be brought to justice. Anticipating his own arrest and imprisonment, Duch said, "It is okay. They have my body. Jesus has my soul."

Duch surrendered to authorities and eventually was put on trial before a tribunal for crimes against humanity: murder and torture. He didn't hide from his past as other Khmer Rouge killers were trying to do.

His testimony made headlines around the world because of his clear-cut confession of his offenses. "I am responsible for the crimes committed at S–21, especially the torture and execution of the people there," he told the five-judge international panel. "May I be permitted to apologize to the survivors of the regime and families of the victims who had loved ones who died brutally at S–21."[20]

At one point, with his consent, Duch was taken in handcuffs to face his accusers. He collapsed in tears, saying, "I ask for your forgiveness. I know that you cannot forgive me, but I ask you to leave me the hope that you might."

Convicted of his crimes, Duch is locked in a prison in Phnom Penh for the rest of his life. The ruling is final.

The judicial system allows no appeal.

A TRUE CONVERSION?

Christopher LaPel and the lay pastor he knew as Hang Pin, now unmasked as the infamous Duch, finally came face-to-face in 2008. Duch had already spent nine years in military detention awaiting trial. A lawyer for the international tribunal had arranged the meeting at Duch's prison.

I tried to put myself in Christopher's position. *What would I say to Duch? What words would suffice? How would I act toward him?*

"What was the very first thing you said to him?" I asked Christopher.

"I said, 'Before we start, I want to tell you that I love you as my brother in Christ. I forgive you for what you've done to my family.'"

"It was as easy as that?" I asked.

He shook his head. "No, not easy—necessary. I had a long time to think and pray about this beforehand. How could I receive forgiveness from Christ for my sins but at the same time refuse to forgive someone for their sins—no matter how evil?"

"How did he respond?"

"In his eyes, I saw tears. As for me, I felt joy and peace in that moment. I felt liberated."

"What happened then?"

"We prayed together, and after that, we praised God and I served him communion. I read the Bible out loud from the twenty-third Psalm."

The familiar passage came to my mind: "The LORD is my shepherd, I lack nothing ... You prepare a table before me in the presence of my enemies ..."

I asked, "Did you talk about what happened at S–21?"

"No, I'm his pastor, not his prosecutor. Duch told me, 'The Holy Spirit has convicted my heart. I have to tell the world what I've done to my people. I will tell the truth, and the truth will set me free.'"

Since then, whenever Christopher makes one of his journeys to Cambodia, he goes to the prison to meet with Duch. Christopher is one of the few visitors allowed to see Duch. He has brought him Cambodian Bibles, a book of worship songs, and a communion set. Each Sunday, as part of his own private worship session in a prison with no other Christians, Duch serves himself communion.

Duch is joyful. He is peaceful. Yes, he carries the weight of his crimes, but he is so thankful for God's grace. He is sharing Jesus with the guards and the other prisoners, who are former Khmer Rouge. He tells them there's forgiveness available for them, as well.

He told Christopher, "I'm not a prisoner; I'm a free man. I rejoice every day of my life. I deserve death. I deserve this punishment. But I have Jesus, and so I have love. If I had Jesus before, I never would have done what I did. I never knew about his love."

Christopher was called to testify at Duch's trial. The panel of judges seemed fascinated by Christopher's description of how Duch has changed.

Christopher described how Duch had admitted he was a sinner, received Christ as Lord and Savior, and was baptized. He talked about the Christian concepts of forgiveness, grace, and conversion. He discussed the value of reconciliation.

"For ninety minutes," Christopher told me, "they allowed me to preach the Good News."

At one point, a judge leaned forward and asked the question on everyone's mind: "Was this a true conversion?"

Christopher had sworn on the Bible to tell the truth.

He replied simply: "Yes."

BREAKING THE CYCLE

Nine out of ten people in Cambodia are Buddhist.[21] Duch's fate would be clear under Buddhist theology — his sins would follow him as bad karma. He would have to try to work off the bad karma over many successive lifetimes. One Buddhist monk has predicted that Duch will return in the next life in the form of a bug.[22]

To a lot of people, that sounds like justice, given the brutality of Duch's crimes.

"Maybe that would be justice," Christopher said. "But grace is not fair. And everyone should be grateful for that, not just Duch. If God were to deny Duch grace by drawing a line and saying, 'No more,' then who's to say where the line might be drawn next time?

"Jesus' death has infinite value because he's an infinite God.

The Case for Grace

His death was enough to cover all the sins of the world. If we say some sin is too terrible, then we're saying Jesus fell short in his mission. Grace is only grace if it's available even to the Duchs of the world. In fact," Christopher said, straightening himself in his chair, "here's a difficult thing for us to comprehend: God loves Duch as much as he loves you and me."

Think about that. I find it hard to accept.

It's easy for me to think I don't need as much grace as Duch does. After all, I've never tortured anybody. Yet I conveniently forget my various forms of idolatry, the ungodly language that occasionally slips out, my daily failure to follow God's teachings. No, Duch doesn't deserve grace, but I don't deserve grace either—and neither do you. For each of us, it's a gift.

Thankfully, that grace and forgiveness is available to everyone who is willing to receive it.

I asked Christopher what people in Cambodia think about Duch. Do they agree with that monk's comment, or do they believe that even Duch could be redeemed?

"Many are hearing of his strong faith and saying, 'Look how God can change a life,'" Christopher said. "They are surprised he would admit his guilt and humbly ask forgiveness. They're saying, 'Look at these Christians—they are forgiving. Why can't we do that, too?' I think, in the end, this will help the churches in Cambodia. God is opening up hearts and minds to see that Jesus is love and that he can bring healing and hope.

"That's very important," he continued, "because grace is unknown in Buddhism. So many Cambodians hold on to their hatred and anger. They don't know how to release it. Someday, it might erupt into another era of violence. Maybe if Cambodians can learn about forgiveness through Duch's story, it can break the cycle. What else but grace can do that?"

CHAPTER SIX

The Street Person

According to a man named Cody Huff, one touch made all the difference in his life. A single, simple gesture — human contact from one person — started a process that resulted in grace going viral as Cody "caught" it and passed it on. This is his story.

He was digging in a dumpster behind a pizzeria in Las Vegas, hunting for half-eaten chicken wings and scraps of crust, when suddenly the hopelessness of his situation hit him with full force.

It's come to this — I'm eating out of garbage cans. I'm sleeping in the dirt. I'm filthy and I stink and I'm starving to death. And there's no way out. Oh God, there's no future and no hope. Why are you doing this to me? He collapsed in the trash and began to sob. The tears wouldn't stop.

"If I had owned a gun, I would have put it in my mouth and pulled the trigger," Cody was saying to me. "I swear to you, I would have. I'd lost everything. I was an addict. I'd been in and out of jail. I was homeless. I was shunned. Every last ounce of my dignity was gone. I hated myself. I hated my life. And I hated God."

Now, tears pooled once more. "That was the day I hit bottom. I couldn't go any lower." He dug into his back pocket for a handkerchief. "I was so hungry. I was so exhausted. I was so desperate. I was so ashamed. I had nothing left. Do you know what that feels like? I *had* nothing, and I *was* nothing."

Cody was headed toward destruction. He had been a burglar, a drug dealer, a counterfeiter, and a scammer. He had been beaten, shot at, and stabbed. He had sat atop mountains of cash and frittered it all away on meth and heroin.

His life was in a tailspin — and then it all came down to one moment. No, not *that* moment — not the time he was crying bitterly in the garbage. That seemed like the end, only it turned out it wasn't.

There was a brief, unlikely, spontaneous experience of grace yet to come. And through it came an insight for me on how to bring grace to others.

GLADIATOR SCHOOL

With bristly gray hair, a goatee, and arms decorated with tattoos, Cody was sitting across from me in an armless upholstered chair. His face was weathered, his voice raspy at times — the effects of being kicked in the throat after being jumped by a gang years ago. He looked every bit of his sixty years — and more. And yet, his tone was humble and his spirit meek as he talked with painful candor about a life that was one long and frightening slide toward hell.

"My dad? No, I never knew my father. He was nineteen when he got my mom pregnant. She was fourteen. They were forced into getting married, and then he took off," Cody said.

"Did you ever connect with him?" I asked.

"Many years later, I called him and asked if he ever wondered what had become of me," Cody replied. "He told me, 'No, not really.'"

Cody's mother dropped out of school and worked as a waitress and then a bank teller in a small town north of Sacramento. Cody doesn't like to discuss the physical abuse he endured and says only that life was chaotic and traumatic. He started smoking marijuana as a way of escape when he was twelve years old. The next year, he ran away to live in a hippie commune in San Francisco.

"There I was — thirteen years old, selling an underground newspaper on the streets, and chipping in money for food and drugs. Anywhere from fourteen to eighteen people lived in the house. We had the *real* stuff — Orange Sunshine, LSD – 25, magic mushrooms, mescaline. I've probably taken LSD 200 times in my life."

The authorities found him four months later, and Cody spent his first stint in juvenile hall. Soon after he got out, he was arrested for his first felony, a hit-and-run car accident. He was sent to the California Youth Authority. Basically, it was a prison for kids. He was fifteen years old.

"We called it Gladiator School," he said. "They would give you a garbage can lid and a shank, and then you were on your own. I learned how to fight, how to make drugs, and how to sell drugs there. It was an education in crime. I was a fast learner. And when I got out a year later, I started putting all of that education to work."

FROM JAIL TO NURSING TO VEGAS

It didn't take long for Cody to become a thriving business-man — in the illicit drug trade.

"I had great products: cocaine, psychedelics, marijuana. And I offered excellent customer service. I even had a pipeline for selling drugs to the inmates at Soledad Prison. Pretty soon, I was making thousands of dollars a week and living on the beach near Monterey. It was all parties and rock concerts. I was buying whatever I wanted, whenever I wanted. And then I did something incredibly stupid.

"I put a needle in my arm."

"Heroin?"

"Yeah. Within six months, I was going through ten bags a day. You get to the point with heroin that you don't care if you eat or if you have a place to sleep. All you care about is getting a hit. I began to sell off everything just to buy the drug. Before long, I had lost it all, so I started stealing. We would work with prostitutes by posing as cops and busting in to rob their clients. Once we got a master key to a hotel and stole forty color television sets. When they came to arrest me, I had a hypodermic needle and some heroin in my back pocket. They gave me a year in jail."

At least, I thought to myself, *this forced him to go through detox.* "Did you come out clean?"

"Yeah, I did. It became very clear that half of Monterey was wanting to kill me for the stuff I'd done, so I left with just a few pieces of clothing and headed for San Diego."

"You decided to go straight?"

"Uh, no. I started committing burglaries on homes. I was pretty successful; I went two years without getting caught. I used drugs casually — no heroin — and I only had to break into a house once a week or even once a month. The money was that good. But it all ended when someone saw me go through the window of a place on the beach and called the police. When I came out, they arrested me. With my prior record, the judge gave me one to fifteen years in prison."

"What were you thinking when the judge sentenced you?"

Cody pursed his lips. "I wasn't thinking about the one year; I was fixated on the fifteen years. I thought, *I'm going to be forty by the time I get out. I'll be an old man!* The next morning, I was handcuffed, shackled, and taken by prison bus to the California State Prison in Chino. I was still a kid. I'd been to juvenile hall and jails — but prison? This was the scariest place I'd ever seen. Fortunately, I got through it all right because my underworld connections gave me protection."

Cody was released after a year. He returned to San Diego and moved in with a woman who worked as a private nurse. "Cody, why don't you go to nursing school?" she suggested one day. Amazingly, he agreed, and this high school dropout and convicted felon managed to become a licensed practical nurse.

Somehow he was hired at a prestigious hospital that didn't bother to run a background check. From then on, future employers never questioned his résumé. That credential was a golden ticket.

For four years, he worked legitimate jobs as a nurse. But then he and his girlfriend broke up.

"When I got emotionally upset, I went back to my old friend — heroin," he said. "I went off the deep end. I was desperate to get a new start, so I went to a fresh place — Las Vegas."

"Vegas? Seriously?"

"Yeah, that was another stupid decision," he said. "If you're trying to get off drugs and away from partying, that's the last place in the world you want to go."

"Tell me about your first day there."

"I sat down in a bar. A guy drinking a beer said, 'What are you doing in Vegas?' He looked cool, so I said, 'I've been doing too many drugs, and to tell you the truth, I'm feeling sick right now.' He said, 'Do you want to get well?' I said, 'Do you know somebody?' He said, '*Know* somebody? I *am* somebody!'

"We walked two blocks away, and he sold me heroin. That started me on another slide that went real bad, real quick. I started doing drugs, partying, spending my savings from nursing like it was going out of style. After three months, I was running low on cash."

That's when Cody learned how to really make money — literally. "I got into a counterfeiting ring," he explained. "We were making silver dollars out of lead. No kidding, you couldn't tell them from the real thing. We would make a thousand of them and use them in slot machines. We were trading our phony money for their real money — and then we'd buy drugs. Above all else, I had to feed my habit."

After two years, the FBI, the police, and Nevada gaming

authorities came after Cody. They posted his picture all over the city. Figuring it was only a matter of time until they arrested him, Cody turned himself in. He was sentenced to another year in jail.

Cody sighed. "It was just endless," he said. "I would gain everything, then lose it all. I'd get off drugs, then I'd get hooked again. I'd work a legitimate job as a nurse, then I'd get back into crime. In all, I've done eight years in prison. That's a long time behind bars, Lee, *eight years*. That does something to your heart. It becomes tough as leather."

HOW TO BE HOMELESS

Out of jail once more, Cody got a job doing in-home nursing care for an eighty-year-old woman in exchange for room and board. Fed up with how his life was going, he recognized this as a chance to go straight. Soon, he was cooking her meals, cleaning her house, mowing her lawn, and taking her to doctor appointments. He was off drugs, and she began paying him a salary.

"Over time, this woman became like a grandmother to me," he said. "You see, I never had a family. I never knew what it was like to have someone just love you. I told her everything about my past and said, 'So, Mimi, this is what you're dealing with.' Mimi, it turned out, was a Christian, and she said, 'You know what? God forgives you, and I forgive you.'"

The more Mimi encouraged him, the more he wanted to serve her. He was her caretaker and surrogate grandson at the same time. On his days off, Cody turned his love of fishing into a second job. He won professional bass tournaments and earned a whole lot of prize money. His life seemed to be healthy for the first time. Then Mimi started going downhill, especially mentally.

"I loved Mimi, and I had to watch her lose her mind. It broke my heart. I couldn't take it. I knew I should have been stronger, but I never loved a patient like that and didn't know what to do.

"One day, I was at a friend's house, and he lit up a pipe to smoke crack. I said, 'Give me a hit.' He looked at me and said,

'Cody, you don't want a hit of this.' I said, 'Yeah, I do.' Before long, I was smoking a thousand dollars of crack a night. It was worse than heroin. Then Mimi died, and I really went off the deep end. I didn't care about anything. It was all about girls and crack, that's all."

Within eighteen months, Cody burned through all his savings. He was kicked out of his house. That began nearly a year of home-lessness on the gritty streets of Las Vegas.

"I had nowhere to go. I had no money. I had a drug habit. I didn't know what to do," he recalled. "I didn't even know how to be homeless. I filled a backpack with some jeans, T-shirts, sweatshirts, a few pairs of socks, some toothpaste, and a toothbrush. I didn't even think to take a sleeping bag.

"The first day, I went around and interviewed homeless people. I'd say, 'My name is Cody, and I've never been homeless. Could I ask you a few questions? Like, where do you clean up? Where do you go to the bathroom? Where's the best part of town to be? How do you eat?'

"I slept in a dirt field that first night, and when I woke up, I was really hungry. I walked up to a man and said, 'Sir, could you spare a couple of bucks so I could get a hamburger? I haven't eaten since yesterday.' And with that, I just burst into tears. He told me, 'Go get a job!' and I started cussing at him.

"I couldn't bring myself to beg anymore. It was so demean-ing. So I hustled a couple of bucks and bought a bottle of window cleaner. As people drove into a shopping center, I'd say, 'Could I clean the windows of your car for you?' They'd ask, 'What do you charge?' I'd say, 'Just make a donation.' That's how I took care of myself when I was homeless.

"I would work night and day for three straight days without a break. By then, I'd have forty or fifty dollars in my pocket. I'd take a bus to Fremont Street, where all the crack dealers were, and I'd buy fifty bucks worth of crack."

"How long did it take to smoke it?"

He shrugged. "Ten minutes."

"Then what?"

"I'd get back on the bus, go to another shopping center, and work again for three days straight. By then, I was exhausted. I'd fall asleep in a park. Flies were all over me; it didn't matter. Every once in a while, a Catholic priest would bring sandwiches to the homeless there. At eleven in the evening, when the park closed, all the homeless would go over to a dirt field behind the police department. I had blankets that I found in garbage cans."

Before long, he hit bottom. That's when he was scrounging around in the dumpster behind the pizzeria, scavenging for anything edible, and he was overcome with desperation. There seemed to be no path out.

"I sat there and just cried and cried. It was bad enough being homeless, but you lose your self-respect and self-esteem little by little. The world makes you feel like you don't matter. You just want to die."

"THEY DON'T CARE"

Once he went to the mental health department and said, "I'm crazy. I need help." They said, "We can't do anything for you. You're a dope addict. Get out of here!"

"I tried to look for a job. I'd shave. I'd get a clean T-shirt. I'd go to the bathroom in the park and try to bathe. They had a nozzle where you could get water for your dog, and I'd use that to shampoo my hair. But I still looked horrible.

"I'd walk into a business and say, 'I'm going to be real honest with you—I'm homeless. I can't even feed myself. I'll do anything—I'll paint, clean, do your dishes, wash your car, pull weeds.' And they'd say, 'You've gotta be kidding! Get outta here before I call the police!'

"It got to the point in the last four or five months of being homeless that I just didn't care anymore. It didn't matter to me if my teeth fell out or if I smelled. I dropped to 135 pounds. If I took off my shirt, you could count my ribs. I wore pants with a thirty-inch waist, and I had to take a shoestring and tie the loops together just to get them to stay up. I was getting busted pretty regularly for jaywalking, vagrancy, smoking crack in public, trespassing."

"How did people treat you?"

"Horribly. If I was walking across the street, some cars would speed up, like they were trying to hit me."

"Seriously?"

"Yeah. You know the old saying, 'You treat me like a dog'? Man, you know what? Dogs are treated a whole lot better than homeless people. I remember how it feels when people don't really care if you lie down and die. Honestly, they don't care."

I was feeling guilty about my attitude toward the homeless people I had encountered throughout the years. "Did you find any generous people?" I asked.

"Every once in a while. I remember being in a grocery store parking lot when a woman in a red car drove in. I don't have anything wrong with my leg, but when I was washing windows I would limp. So I limped up to the car and said, 'Excuse me, ma'am, could I clean your windows?' She said, 'Well, I just got my car detailed, so I don't need that. But are you hungry?' I said, 'I'm starving.'

"She reached into her purse and pulled out a five-dollar gift certificate from a hamburger place. It was a lifesaver. I went and had a couple of hamburgers, french fries, a soft drink. I spent all but twelve cents of that certificate. Man, that felt good.

"After months without a shower, wearing the same clothes day after day, I began to smell terrible. When I'd come back to the field at night, I reeked so bad that the other homeless people could smell me thirty feet away. They started yelling at me. 'Cody, you stink!' 'Cody, get some clean clothes!' 'Cody, you need a bath!'

"Finally, the guy next to me told me about Central Christian Church."

That name sounded familiar. "That's where Jud Wilhite is pastor," I said.

"That's right. They would let the homeless come and take a

shower, shave, get clean clothes, have breakfast, and go to a service if you wanted. That sounded good to me — all except for the service — so I said I'd go with that guy the next day, which was Sunday. We got up at four in the morning and walked seven miles to get there."

"Was it worth it for the meal and clothes?"

He chuckled. "Oh, it was worth it, all right, but not just for those things," he said. "You see, this was the day that changed my life."

THE HUG

Cody was waiting in line for a shower at Central Christian. Several homeless men were milling around, so he didn't feel conspicuous. Tables were set with free coffee and food.

That's when a volunteer named Michelle came in. Middle-aged and petite, Michelle surveyed the room then walked over to him and said, "Sir?"

Cody turned and found Michelle looking him straight in the eyes.

"Sir," she said simply, "you look like you need a hug."

Cody couldn't believe it. *A hug?* His hair was matted. His beard was scraggly. His clothes were dirty and stained. His teeth were rotting in his mouth. *A hug?* He shook his head. "Ma'am, I haven't taken a shower in three months," he said. "I smell horrible."

Michelle smiled. "You don't smell to me," she said. And then she wrapped her arms around him. Again, she looked him in the eyes. "Do you know," she said, "that Jesus loves you?"

Jesus can't love me, Cody was thinking. *I'm homeless. Jesus can't love me. I'm a drug addict. I'm a bad man.*

"Jesus loves you," she repeated.

What can God accomplish through a hug? Are three words about Jesus sufficient to redeem a lost soul? How much can one expression of love straighten a path that has been crooked from the start?

At that moment, in an instant, something spiritual sparked

inside of Cody. To this day, years later, he can't talk about it without his voice cracking.

"Plain and simple, that was the pivotal moment of my life," he told me. "It was like a personal encounter with Jesus. It was love, pure love. She didn't care what I looked like or how much I smelled. It was like Jesus himself was standing in front of me and saying, 'Cody, I love you.'

"At the time in my life when I was the least lovable, when everyone shunned me, when there was no hope of getting out of the mess I was in, when I smelled so bad that even other homeless people didn't want to be around me — there she was, with this simple expression of the grace of God. And something happened in my heart."

"What was it?"

Cody glanced off to the side, gathering his thoughts, then looked back at me. He started to say something but stopped. Then he said, "Honestly, Lee, I don't know. All I can say is that it was a spiritual moment. It was a hug, but it was more than that — it was what the hug was saying to me. *I accept you. I care about you. You matter to me. You have value and worth. You have dignity as a human being.*

"That was the first time in so long that anyone cared if I lived or died. Even *I* didn't care anymore. I think that's why I kept doing drugs; I was hoping that the next hit would stop my heart.

"And then," he said, "this hug." He snapped his fingers. "It changed everything."

A PRAYER IN THE DIRT

Cody got his shower that day at Central Christian, put on some clean clothes, ate a good breakfast, and then sat in on a Bible study.

"Right away, something was different," he told me. "It was like a light switch had been turned on. The more I heard about Jesus, the more I wanted to hear. Then Michelle said, 'Do you want to go to church?' I said, 'Well, yeah, but the building might fall down!'

"We went to the service, and I sat in the highest row, way up in the balcony, in the dark, where nobody could see me. The pastor, Jud, got up and said some older ladies had been complaining that the music the kids were playing in church was too loud. 'I'm going to tell you how I feel about this,' Jud said. 'If those kids are playing music and worshipping Jesus, I say turn it up!' And I thought, *Yes, this is my kind of church!*"

Starting that day, Cody couldn't hear enough about Jesus. He trudged back and forth to the church. He started cutting back on the drugs. He attended the church's ministry for the homeless. Everything came together three weeks later in the park he called home.

"I didn't really know anything about the Bible, except God loves me, Jesus died for me, I'm a sinner, forgiveness is available — and I wanted it," he told me.

"I didn't even know how to pray. I got on my knees, with my face in the dirt, crying like a baby, and I just poured out my heart. I said, 'God, I'm so tired. I'm tired of the drugs. Please, take them away from me. It's like I've been driving my own car and all I do is get into head-on crashes. Why don't you drive? I'm sorry for the way I've lived. I want to surrender my life to you. God, please make me a new man.'

"I can't even tell you how long I prayed — maybe ten or fifteen minutes — and when I said, 'Amen,' I was filled with the most incredible peace I had ever felt. It was like a wave in the ocean, like when I used to go surfing and a wave would *whoosh* over me. I felt clean for the first time. I didn't know where all this was leading, but starting right then, God took away my desire for drugs."

"That doesn't happen for everyone," I said.

"I know. It can be a process and a struggle. But for me, everything began to change right away. In fact, that evening, there were about forty of us sleeping in that field. Before then, nobody had ever offered me drugs for free. That night, they kept waking me and offering me crack pipes. My best friend said, 'Here, Cody; I just put ten dollars on this.' I said, 'Steve, get away from me. I quit. I'm done. Dude, I've turned over my life to Jesus Christ.' He said, 'What do you mean, Cody?' I said, 'I don't know what it all looks like, but I'm his now. I don't do that stuff anymore.'

"Three weeks later, I got baptized. I was scared to death in front of all those people, but Michelle was there. She said, 'Cody, ain't nothing can keep me away from seeing you baptized.'

"I kept going to the Bible study every week and church every week. I couldn't get enough of the Bible. I started telling everyone about Jesus, even though I didn't really know that much about him. I'd be holding little Bible studies in the field, using a pocket Bible."

Cody became a volunteer at the church. The cook would make him enormous sandwiches for lunch. "I can't eat all this," Cody would say. The cook would hand him some plastic wrap. "Then you've got dinner for later," he replied. Pretty soon, through a connection at the church, Cody was offered a job and a place to live. For the first time in years, he was gainfully employed and self-supporting.

He kept serving in the church's homeless ministry. One time, they were providing food to a group of homeless people who lived under a bridge, and Cody saw another volunteer who looked famil-iar. He had seen that face somewhere before. *Where was it?* Oh, yeah, she was the woman in the red car who had given him the food certificate when he was homeless.

He introduced himself and told her his story. "I'm sorry — I give out so many of those coupons that I don't remember you," she said. "But I'm thrilled you're a Christian now!"

She's a nice lady, Cody thought. Her name was Heather.

NEW LIFE IN THE PARK

On a balmy spring evening during a trip to Las Vegas, I was watching as dozens of homeless men and women gathered under a big gazebo in a park. A man with a broken leg arrived in a shop-ping cart pushed by a friend. Volunteers were barbecuing chicken.

Everyone's attention was riveted on the enthusiastic gray-haired man in a T-shirt and jeans, clutching a Bible in one hand and pointing off into the distance with the other.

"I used to sleep in the dirt not far from here," Cody was saying into a microphone. "Then a woman gave me a hug and told me that Jesus loves me. There she is, over there — sitting in the back. It was a moment of grace for me. And friends, I don't care what you've been through; Jesus will take you in his arms too. He will hug you like she hugged me. Only with Jesus, he will never let you go."

Cody is an ordained minister now at Hope Church in Las Vegas. He serves as the volunteer director of Broken Chains, a ministry that helps feed and house the homeless people of Las Vegas. It's supported by a number of churches and local businesses, including a retailer that used to call the cops on Cody when he was a vagrant in their parking lot. Cody gets invited to address training classes of police officers, like the ones who used to harass him when he would sleep in the park.

WANT TO KNOW MORE?

Find out about Broken Chains at
BrokenChainsOutreach.com.

These days, Cody holds regular events in that same park, where Broken Chains offers free meals, music, and spiritual encouragement. And the woman wielding the tongs as she grills the chicken? That's Heather, the one with the red car. She is Cody's wife now.

After Cody shared his story to the crowd that evening, people lined up so Heather could serve them dinner. Later, I found myself standing among the picnic tables and chatting with Cody, who was watching with satisfaction as his guests devoured their food.

He chuckled. "You know, when I prayed to Jesus on my knees in the dirt, I told him I'd follow him even if he wanted me to stay in

The Case for Grace

this park the rest of my life," Cody told me. "Little did I know, that was his plan."

These are his people, this congregation of crack addicts and drunks, the unshaven, unwashed, unemployed, and unwanted. I think that night Cody must have hugged them all.

I strolled over to Michelle. She was standing in the back, taking everything in.

"Did you think when you gave Cody a hug that it would lead to all this?" I asked.

Her smile was modest. "No — who could have foreseen this?"

"Why did you do it?" I asked. "When Cody was dirty and smelly and homeless, why did you offer him a hug?"

She looked at me like it was the stupidest question ever — and maybe it was. "Because he looked like he needed one," she replied. "That's what Jesus would do, isn't it?"

No doubt that's true. But what about me? Back on that day, would I have shaken Cody's hand or given him a bear hug or even a pat on the back? Would I have gone out of my way to tell him about Jesus? Would I have seen the potential for redemption and transformation? Would I have given him the dignity he deserved?

I thought about those questions for a while, and I didn't much like my answers. How many times had I seen someone like Cody on the street and thought of him more as a problem to be solved than a person to be loved? How often had I kept grace to myself?

I said good-bye to Michelle and scanned the crowd under the gazebo. I decided to walk over to the scruffy young man who had arrived in a shopping cart, his leg in a cast. He was sitting by himself on outskirts of the group.

"My name is Lee," I said. "What's yours?"

"They call me Spider." His voice was hoarse.

Hesitantly, I draped my arm around his shoulder. "Well, Spider, tell me your story," I said. "And then let me tell you about a friend who has changed my life. His name is Jesus, and he loves you."

CHAPTER SEVEN

The Faker

Posers. Nobody likes them. But what do you do if everyone expects you to be a "good Christian," and you aren't? Or tougher yet—what if you really *want* to be a "good Christian," but deep down you know you're far from it? Do you put up a front, or is there another option?

Andrew Palau would say the only good option is repentance. And he'd tell you that he found it out the hard way.

Andrew is the third of four sons born to Luis and Pat Palau. In his early years, Luis translated for Billy Graham. Luis went on to become one of his generation's most famous and effective evangelists. His outreach festivals, books, and radio programs have now reached a billion people in seventy-five countries.[23]

That's Luis. Andrew is a different story.

When Andrew was born, his grandmother made a prediction: "This one is going to be an evangelist." But those hopes evaporated early. Though young Andrew put on a Christian front, he was faking it. He couldn't care less about Jesus. And pretty soon, his faking wasn't fooling anyone. He fell into drinking and smoking dope. He was kicked out of a Christian university. He flitted from girl to girl. He was having a good time, but he was going nowhere.

EVERY DECISION A BAD ONE

"I was a fool," Andrew says now as he looks back on how he used to be. "Proverbs has a lot to say about foolish people. Just go down the list — that was me.

Read it here

The Old Testament book of Proverbs describes fools this way:

- Fools hate wisdom.
- Fools are self-satisfied.
- Fools bring grief to their parents.
- Fools lack common sense.
- Fools are full of pride.
- Fools practice deception.
- Fools reject discipline.
- Fools won't take advice.

And that's just the start!

Read some of the descriptions in Proverbs 1:7, 1:32, 10:18, 10:21, 10:23, 12:23, 14:3, 14:8, 14:9, 15:5, 17:21, 23:9, 30:32.

"I squandered every opportunity. I took the path of least resistance, and I stumbled through life drunk or stoned or both. Just about every decision I made was wrong. Everything was about *me*: having fun, chasing women, partying with friends, getting into trouble. It was a competition to see who could do the craziest stuff and laugh about it the next day. If that's not being a fool, then I don't know what is."

I was taken aback by his blunt assessment of himself, which, frankly, sounded a lot like me in my early years. "What was driving you?" I asked. "Were your parents hypocrites? Did your father neglect you or abuse you or wound you emotionally?"

"No, nothing like that. I can't blame anyone else. I wanted to be cool so I'd be accepted by all the girls and the right guys in the right cliques. I was selfish, self-centered, self-indulgent—and I was rebellious, although not because I was angry at God."

"Did you think Christianity was true?"

"Well, this is embarrassing, but I thought it probably *was* true. The thing is, I just didn't care. I loved my sin too much."

"You must have done a good job of hiding it from your parents," I said.

"Yeah, I put on a show of being Christian. I would say all the right things—and when I had to, I'd lie to get myself out of trouble. I did everything a good evangelist's boy was supposed to do: I was part of the church's youth group, I memorized Bible verses, I went to missions conferences, and I attended church every Sunday."

"What did you think of church?"

"I kind of liked it."

"Really?"

"Sure," he replied. "People were very friendly. Besides, a lot of my party friends attended church. I didn't want to cause any hassle for my parents, so I just tried to move along in the Christian world. I played it pretty well."

LOOKING FOR TROUBLE

Early in life, Andrew began flirting with trouble to gain attention from the crowd he wanted to impress. First, there was petty vandalism and other reckless behavior, like blowing up jugs of gasoline on highways at night to startle drivers, igniting Molotov cocktails in the schoolyard, and building bigger and more powerful pipe bombs. Then came theft and drinking, with Andrew and his friends stealing beer and alcohol from the garages and liquor cabinets of their neighbors. Pretty soon came marijuana. "In high school, we'd smoke dope on the way to school, at lunch, and then after school," Andrew said. "We would party every chance we could get, usually at a house when parents were out of town."

"Did you ever get caught?"

"Sometimes. One time in high school, we were drinking, and I crashed a car into someone's front yard. I got a ticket for hit-and-run driving. That's a felony, but I managed to get out of it. Usually, I could weasel my way out of trouble. Getting away with things made me even bolder the next time."

After high school, he went to conservative Biola University in Southern California. "There I was at a new place where nobody knew me. I could have made a fresh start, but I stuck to what I knew: partying and drinking."

He lasted a year until Biola "invited" him to "seek success elsewhere." He transferred to the University of Oregon in Eugene, a more liberal school, where he majored in English literature and dabbled in cocaine and hallucinogenic drugs.

"By then, I was really out of control," he said. "Nobody was looking over my shoulder, so I pushed the limits. I was manipulative and deceitful to the women I was dating. On weekends, my friends and I would go to isolated sand dunes at the beach, build a fire, play music, drink beer, trip on acid, and spend the night. Eventually, our fraternity was banned from campus after we torched an old Volkswagen Beetle that belonged to one of our frat brothers."

His classes weren't going much better. "I liked people to think I was an intellectual, but actually, I was shallow. I knew just enough about literature to fool someone who didn't know any better," he said.

Andrew dropped out of school and went to Europe. He worked at an upscale clothing store in Wales. He took time off to bum around the Continent, smoke hashish, and stow away on a ship. Then, he moved to Northern Ireland, where he worked at a furniture store.

THE PANHANDLER AND THE NIGHTCLUB

Fast forward a few years. By now, Andrew was living in Boston. He remained as far from God as ever.

"I was always partying, which was a little embarrassing for someone my age," he said. "I was using it to mask all the guilt and shame in my life. I didn't like to go to bed sober, because then I'd be haunted by memories of all the people I had hurt or deceived or used. And there was anxiety—fear of the future, fear of the world, fear of eternity."

"When did you hit bottom?"

"Two things happened. Some friends and I were out drinking one night, and we got into a shouting match with a panhandler on a sidewalk. After a while, he lay down to sleep. I can't believe we did this, but we started kicking him, repeatedly."

He grimaced. "I mean, how low can a person get—kicking a homeless person?" he said. "Really, I'm ashamed to even tell the story. How did I sink so low that I thought that was okay to do? That was probably my lowest point. And then something bizarre happened in a nightclub that really shook me."

"A nightclub?"

"Yeah, a huge, warehouse-type place—a techno-pop dance club. It was pretty dark, and people were everywhere. I was headed to the bathroom when a guy sort of grabbed me and said, 'You're a believer.' I said, 'What are you talking about?' He repeated, 'You're a believer, right?'"

"Was it someone you knew?" I asked.

"No, that was the odd part. I was thinking maybe he recognized me from church when I was a kid, or maybe he was a friend of my dad's. I thought, *Oh no, this is awful. This guy thinks I'm a Christian, and he wants to talk about it.* I was desperate to get away from him. So I said, 'Yeah, I'm a believer,' hoping to satisfy him and get out of a conversation."

"How did he respond?"

"He said, 'I knew it. You're a follower of Satan, right?' And he smiled and walked away into the crowd. I started protesting, saying, 'No, no, no,' but he was gone. It was chilling to me."

I pictured the bizarre scene. "What did you make of it?"

"I was haunted by it. What did he see in me that made him think I was a follower of Satan? Or could this have been some sort of supernatural encounter? It seemed demonic, like I was engaging something very dark. I wondered whether my lifestyle of drugs and booze had opened a gateway into another world. And certainly, that's possible."

He shook his head, dismayed with himself. "But like so many other times in my life, after a while, I simply moved on, down the same twisted road I had been traveling all along."

A DECISION, BUT HESITATION

Luis Palau can be clever. He waited until the winter temperature in Boston was unbearably cold, and then he called to invite Andrew to one of his evangelistic rallies. When Andrew said he wasn't interested, Luis casually let it be known that the event would be in Jamaica. After Luis agreed to set up a marlin-fishing trip for him, Andrew started to pack his bags.

Andrew ended up staying with a Jamaican businessman and his family, which included son Chris and daughter Wendy. As Andrew hung around with them and their friends, he was amazed — and intrigued — by their fresh and enthusiastic faith. They seemed to be living "life to the full" like he had always heard his parents talk about.

Read it here

This is what Jesus says about living life to the full in John 10:10:

> "The thief comes only to steal and kill
> and destroy; I have come that they may
> have life, and have it to the full."

"They were fun and normal, warm and friendly. And they were sold out to Christ in a very attractive and radical way," Andrew recalled. "Jesus seemed so real and present to them. I was listening as they told others about how God had healed their addictions and restored their relationships—and I was thinking, *This is what I need! I can't keep pretending that my shame and guilt aren't dogging me. Something has got to happen*."

On three of the five nights when Luis was preaching at the Kingston National Stadium, Andrew attended with his new friends.

"I always respected Dad and the sincerity of his message," Andrew told me. "On the last night of the crusade, I went with a receptive attitude. I really wanted to hear the voice of the God who had so completely changed the lives of these new friends of mine."

"And did you?"

"Well, as I sat there and listened, it struck me that Dad's message was different than ever before. It was like he was picking on me. He really went after me. And then I realized: this was the same message he almost always gave. The difference was that this time I was willing to really listen.

"When he gave the invitation to receive Christ, I found myself saying in my spirit, *Lord, this is what I want. Please come into my life. I'm going in a new direction. I want heaven, and I want to do the right thing. Everything I say I hate but I can't stop doing—I want to stop doing it. Everything I say I want to do but can't seem to do—I want to do it*. At that moment, I determined to stop drinking, break off my inappropriate relationships, and start going to church."

SAME OLD, SAME OLD

Andrew's friends in Boston were surprised when he told them he was now a Christian. They watched warily as he went to church and started to clean up his life. But the "new" Andrew lasted only a month.

"One night, I went out with some friends to a bar—not to drink, but just to hang out with them," Andrew said to me. "Pretty soon, I had a beer. Then another. Then six, plus three straight shots. And I started smoking dope. Before long, I was involved again with some of the girls I knew I should be avoiding."

"So everything fell apart?"

"Completely. I embarrassed myself—and the Lord. My friends were laughing at me. I was ashamed and humiliated. My life started to spiral downward again. I kept thinking, *How could my commitment to God have been so real to me—and now this? How could I have been so sincere and yet fail so badly? And what was I supposed to do now?*"

"Looking back, what do you think happened?"

"I didn't really want God to rule all of my life. I wanted to hang on to the partying and the so-called 'fun' stuff. As I look back at it, my prayer in Jamaica was hollow. A salvation prayer doesn't mean much unless you authentically turn from sin and allow God to take over your life. That's what he deserves. I was saying, 'I want all the good things you offer—the forgiveness, the release from guilt, heaven, and all that. And I'll try my hardest to do good to keep you happy and get the things I genuinely desire. Yes, I want you, God, but without giving up Me. Is it a deal?'"

Shaking his head, he said: "God doesn't bargain like that. Not at all."

"LORD, I'M OPEN"

Wendy was the reason Andrew went back to visit Jamaica many months later. He had been captivated by her charm and intrigued by her faith in Christ. When Andrew got together with her and her friends again in the islands, he tried his best to act like a Christian. It didn't take them long to see through his charade.

One of them, Steve, confronted Andrew one evening: "May I ask you something? What's *really* going on with you?"

Andrew was busted. He knew they had discerned that he wasn't following Jesus. So he admitted that he was struggling spiritually and had botched his efforts to lead a better life.

The Case for Grace

"I was surprised that Steve didn't panic or get on my case," Andrew told me. "He said it wasn't unusual to need to grow after an initial decision for Christ. He invited me to pray and read the Bible with him the next morning."

Steve read the opening verses of Romans 12 to Andrew: "Therefore, I urge you, brothers and sisters, in view of God's mercy, to offer your bodies as a living sacrifice, holy and pleasing to God — this is your true and proper worship. Do not conform to the pattern of this world, but be transformed by the renewing of your mind. Then you will be able to test and approve what God's will is — his good, pleasing and perfect will."

As they began to discuss the passage, Andrew was frustrated. He had heard the words, but he just didn't understand what they meant.

"I had absolutely no idea what this passage meant," he told me. "I really wanted to hear from God through his Word. But it was like there was a wall between me and the verses."

Steve continued to try to explain what the apostle Paul was teaching in the passage. At the time, Andrew was thinking to himself, *I tried this Christianity thing, and I failed. I'm not sure what these verses mean when they talk about transformation and renewal — but whatever it is, it certainly isn't happening to me.*

Seeing Andrew's exasperation, Steve offered a solution: "You need to come on a retreat."

He said that every year a group of Christians went on a retreat for a few days of building friendships, prayer, worship, and teaching from the Bible.

Andrew felt drawn to the idea. Silently, he prayed: *Lord, I'm open. Let's face it: I've opened myself up to all the garbage of the world — why wouldn't I open myself up to whatever you have for me?*

"I'll do it," Andrew said to Steve.

CONFESSION AND CLEANSING

At the retreat, Andrew kept praying, *If you're real—if all this is true—then I have to know for sure.* He began begging God for a supernatural encounter. *Lord, just do this one more thing: Reveal yourself to me. Stand before me, and I'll know you're real. You can do that, for sure. You've got the power. Then I'll believe, and I'll never forget.*

Over and over, he asked God to appear. He thought that if God didn't respond, then maybe it was time to give up once and for all.

Despite Andrew's prayers—nothing.

Andrew was ready to give up. But he prayed one more time—a different prayer. *God*, he whispered, *what is keeping me from you?*

Instantly, he was startled by a distinct response he felt in his spirit. *Do you really want to know, Andrew? Finally*, he thought, *God is going to appear to me. Yes, God, of course. What is it? What's keeping me from you?*

Andrew's eyebrows raised as he described to me what happened next.

"Immediately, in a flash, God opened my eyes to what had been keeping us apart. There before me was all the garbage of my life. All of my lying, cheating, stealing, and abusive relationships. All the arrogance and pride. All the addictions and people I had hurt. I saw it all, this pile of sin stacked as high as I could see.

"I was horrified! I gasped and fell on my face. I was heaving with sobs; my tears were falling on the floor. 'God,' I said, 'how could I have been such a fool? Please forgive me! Please take this away! I can't live with it anymore. What hope do I have when all of this garbage is in me?'

"And God's response in that moment was right out of Scripture. *If you confess your sin, Andrew, I am able to forgive you of your unrighteousness. I will clean it out. I will take it as far as the east is from the west. I will remember your sin no more.*

The promises God made to Andrew are the same promises
he makes to you: 1 John 1:9; Psalm 103:12; Isaiah 43:25;
Hebrews 10:17.

"I started confessing as fast as God could bring my sins into
my consciousness. He would unveil them to me, one after the other,
and I would cry out for forgiveness, and he would release them.
He was cleaning me, scrubbing me, scouring me. I saw myself as I
really was, and I was shattered. But by his grace, God was piecing
me back together.

"So there I was, face down on the floor, and some of the guys
came over and put their arms on my shoulder and said, 'This is
your time, Andrew. Make sure you get it all out. Don't try to hide
anything from the Lord.' They brought me to a room and helped me
make my confession.

"After two or three hours, it was over — and it was like God
had flipped on a light in my soul. I felt such incredible relief — an
utter sense of release from all the things that had entrapped me. I
kept thanking God for his grace. And then, out of sheer gratitude, I
whispered, 'I will tell everyone what you have done.' As the words
left me, he replied, *You will* — not in the form of a question, but
more of a statement, like he was sealing his calling on my life."

THE REBEL'S ONLY WAY

"Repentance is the rebel's only path to God. I needed to confess
that I'm wrong and God is right. I needed to see my sin in contrast
with his holiness. I needed his cleansing and leadership of my life.
It's not enough just to pray, *God, make me a better person*. It was
repentance that opened the floodgates of grace for me — and it was
grace that changed my life and eternity."

Andrew has kept his promise to tell everyone what God has
done. He has become an evangelist, like his father. He tells the
story of God's grace at rallies and festivals all around the world.

Sometimes, he speaks to crowds of tens of thousands of people. Other times, he spends time one-on-one with inmates in prison.[24]

Oh, and remember Wendy? She and Andrew have now been married for more than twenty years.

Andrew's story sparked strong memories in me. When my wife, Leslie, became a Christian, I saw the changes in her life. I liked what I saw, but I wasn't at all sure that Christianity was legitimate. I spent nearly two years using my legal training and journalism experience to investigate the validity of Christianity. If God were a mirage or a product of wishful thinking, if Jesus were a legend, a fraud, or simply a crutch for the weak, then I wanted nothing to do with Christianity. But as the evidence began to pile up, I became more and more intrigued. And like Andrew, I finally got to the point where I was wide open spiritually. After all, if God is real, why would I not want to experience him?

On the afternoon of Sunday, November 8, 1981, alone in my bedroom, I finished weighing the evidence and arguments for and against Christianity. At that moment, I reached my personal verdict in the case for Christ. But it was more than just a head decision. At the instant I realized that God is alive and that he is holy and perfect and pure, I became horrified by the corruption in my own soul.

Like Andrew, I had been consumed by pride and self-worship, by alcohol and illicit relationships, by the arrogant disregard of others. At that moment when my eyes were opened to God, all of my sin flooded into my mind like the discharge of a sewer. I wanted to run and hide. Only one thing stopped me — a verse a friend had pointed out to me earlier and which I almost instinctively sought out in that moment: "Yet to all who did receive him, to those who believed in his name, he gave the right to become children of God."

Read it here

The verse that changed my life is John 1:12.

The Case for Grace

Oh God, I'm overwhelmed by my sins. Only your grace can save me. Please cleanse me, change me, lead me, use me.

In ways beyond what I ever imagined, God answered me. Like an orphan named Stephanie and an addict named Jud, like a sinner named Craig and a killer called Duch, like a felon named Cody and a faker named Andrew, I was not only forgiven, but I was also welcomed into the caring family of a Father who would never disappoint. For the next thirty years, my life took a new path of adventure and fulfillment as God opened doors to serve him and others in ways I never could have foreseen.

All because of grace.

CHAPTER EIGHT

Giving and Receiving Grace

i started my search for grace because I needed to learn how to forgive someone who had hurt me — my father. My guess is that you've been in that same place — maybe not with your father, but with someone close to you who has broken your heart. Giving grace is hard.

But my conversation with Andrew brought back memories of all the selfish, arrogant, sinful things I had done over the course of my life. I needed to learn how to forgive myself, too. Sometimes that can be just as hard. If you're honest with yourself, you've also been in that place. There are things in your life that you feel guilty about. Things that make you feel dirty.

How could I take what I'd learned about grace and make it real in my own life? I knew just who to ask: Brad and Heidi Mitchell.

THE JOURNEY TOGETHER

Brad was in the sixth grade when he first met Heidi after a church service. He quickly coined a nickname for her: "Hideous Heidi."

As the best friend of Brad's sister, Heidi was constantly over at Brad's house during the two and a half years he lived in North Dakota. He would tease them mercilessly. When his family moved to Indianapolis, he promptly put Heidi out of his mind.

Then Heidi came to Indiana to visit Brad's sister when Brad was sixteen years old. The girls were giggling in a bedroom as Brad arrived home from his job at a warehouse. He settled into a chair downstairs to read the sports section. That's when Heidi, now fourteen years old, came sweeping through the room.

"Hi, Brad," she said, almost offhandedly.

Brad glanced at her. The words that came out of his mouth were casual: "Hi, Heidi." But inside, he was reeling: *Oh my goodness! Wow! What in the world happened to her?*

Later, he invited her to look at his football photos. Before she left his room, he kissed her. And before the end of the weekend, he actually proposed to her—and she accepted. There they were, sixteen and fourteen, too young for her parents to let her date, and in their minds, they were future husband and wife.

Looking back, Brad said, "She was everything I wanted, so I figured, why not lock this up?" Recalled Heidi, "I knew I wanted to get married someday, and suddenly here was this perfect guy. He had morphed from a junior high dweeb into a high school football player. I thought, *this is great! We can be engaged, and my dad doesn't have to know.*"

They worked out the details. They would date other people as they got older, just to make sure they were right for each other. They would go through the same Bible studies and write letters back and forth about how they were growing spiritually. They would attend the same Christian college. They would get married after his

The Case for Grace

graduation, and he would become an attorney or pursue some other high-paying profession.

Amazingly, just as they planned, everything came to pass — except that Brad didn't become a lawyer. He answered the Holy Spirit's leading and became a pastor.

THE RISE TO SUCCESS

The first church that Brad pastored wasn't much of a congregation at the time, just six families. But over the next several years, the church grew to more than 400. From there, Brad moved to an even larger church. Soon, he was traveling two or three weekends a month to speak somewhere, while Heidi stayed home with their children.

After a few years, Brad seized an opportunity to become senior pastor of a church in Michigan. Again, God seemed to bless his efforts. In a no-growth community, the church expanded from 1,800 people to almost 4,000 in six years. Then he accepted a position in a church in South Carolina. It was contemporary, casual, and had a thriving sports ministry, a great staff, and supportive leaders.

It was taking a long time for Brad and Heidi to sell their home in Michigan so they could move to South Carolina. Their daughter wanted to finish her senior year in high school before the transition, so Brad and Heidi came up with a plan: he would move to the East Coast while she stayed in Michigan. He would fly home to visit for one week every month.

Only, it didn't work for them. Brad became involved with another woman.[25]

FEELING THE WEIGHT

"Even on my way to the first encounter, I knew I should turn around, run the other way, get out," Brad told me. "But I chose to keep doing it. And to make it worse, I had the sense that God wouldn't let this destroy my ministry because it would harm the church."

He shook his head in disgust. "I can't believe I ever thought that! Did I believe that God was somehow going to protect my sin? Sometimes we think we're getting away with something, but God is waiting. Will we repent on our own? Or will we keep at it?

"The fear of us being discovered was just horrible. *Horrible!* When I preached, I felt like a hypocrite. I felt empty. I felt like I was going through the motions — and I was. I had no power. The Holy Spirit wasn't blessing my ministry."

Heidi spoke up. "One weekend after I had moved to South Carolina, I went to church and watched Brad preach. I remember sitting there and thinking, *What's wrong with him?* He had no energy, no passion. Physically, he was hunched over. I thought, *Well, maybe he is tired.* Looking back, I think it was literally the weight of sin bearing down on him."

"The shame, the guilt — you're right, they were so heavy," Brad said. "Every time before I'd get up to preach, I'd confess everything to God — and then I'd confess again and again. And then afterward, I went back to the charade. A part of me had become calloused because I was shutting out the voice of God in my life."

For three months, the adultery dragged on. Then Brad was found out. "It was then that I called a Christian counselor. He said to me, 'You've got to tell Heidi. And when you do, have your suitcase packed and in your car, because it's very likely she's going to tell you to leave.'"

One evening as Brad was standing on one side of the bed and Heidi on the other, he finally said, "There's something I need to talk with you about."

"What is it?" she asked.

He dropped down, almost to his knees, leaning over the bed. "I've been unfaithful to you."

The next moments are a blur. Heidi was in shock. Almost immediately, she vomited. She wouldn't be able to eat for four days. Raw and confusing thoughts flooded into her. *I ought to kill him! I ought to kill myself. He's going to lose his job. Everything will be gone. How will we pay the bills? What about the children?*

Where should I go? What should I do? Can I trust him about anything? Oh, God, I need you now more than ever.

Two days later, Brad met with the leaders of the South Carolina church. Brad resigned and had to endure the disgrace of informing the congregation that Sunday. All his years of preparation for the ministry and his success in the pulpit were dashed.

Brad also had to confess to his son and two daughters, who were devastated by the news. He had to tell Heidi's parents and his own parents. Brad and Heidi had to give up the house where they had been living because they couldn't afford it. For a while, they had nowhere to go.

"One of the worst moments," Heidi said, "was when I asked my counselor if we should be tested for sexually transmitted diseases. He said, 'Absolutely.' So Brad and I went to a doctor's office. It was humiliating to ask the nurse for that test. I was so angry with Brad; I didn't even want to sit next to him. I was thinking, *I've been faithful to you. I was a virgin before you, and now I have to get tested for HIV?* It was embarrassing; it was unfair—"

Brad interjected, "It was one more awful and humiliating consequence of my sin."

Still, while they were telling me all this, I noticed that Heidi had quietly taken Brad's hand. Somehow, against so many odds, they had moved from adultery to reconciliation, from hurt to healing.

I needed to know how.

HEIDI — OFFERING GRACE AFTER BETRAYAL

Heidi made it clear to me that the journey toward full forgiveness began with a single step: the *decision* to forgive.

She had been taught that forgiveness was never optional in the Christian faith; God required it. Forgiving wasn't so hard for small offenses. But what about big offenses?

"My conclusion was that Christians don't get to pick and choose what they want to forgive and what they don't," she said. "The Bible says, 'Forgive as the Lord forgave you.' I didn't see any wiggle room in that. As Christ had forgiven me for my sins, I needed to offer grace to Brad. Otherwise, bitterness would consume me, and bitterness is poison in the soul of a Christian. I didn't know if our marriage could be saved, but I knew I needed to forgive him."

Read it here

Read about forgiving others as God forgave you in Colossians 3:13.

"So forgiveness was a matter of obedience?" I asked.

"Yes. I was committed to following Christ, even when it got hard. My relationship with Brad was already damaged; I didn't want my relationship with God to become strained because I refused to follow him when times were tough."

"Did you feel like forgiving Brad?"

"No, not at all. I was hurting too much. But I was determined to forgive. I knew that if I made the choice to offer forgiveness, the feelings might eventually follow. *Maybe.* But grace is a decision before it's an emotion."

"You make it sound pretty easy."

"Well, it was anything but easy. It was emotionally painful for me to forgive Brad. It was mentally painful. It was physically painful. It was relationally painful. But it didn't compare to the pain Jesus endured for me on the cross when he purchased my forgiveness. In light of what Christ went through, how could I withhold forgiveness?"

Heidi spoke the words of forgiveness out of obedience, and she meant them as much as she could at the time. But it took much longer to *feel* forgiveness toward Brad.

"I was still angry," she said. "But in the Christian life, we can never fully rely on our feelings. Sometimes our emotions can keep us from doing what's right. I had to ask God to help my feelings match the forgiveness that was in my heart. Yeah, the feelings took

The Case for Grace

much longer. That was a process. I told God, 'You're going to have to help me. Mold my heart and mind. Draw me closer to you. Help me to be loving like you are.'"

"And did he answer that prayer?"

"Oh, yeah," Heidi said. "The next year was the biggest growth ever in my spiritual life—I mean, huge. I learned so many life-changing lessons—not just about marriage, but about God and his goodness and his faithfulness and his grace. That part I wouldn't trade for anything. I wouldn't be the person I am today if I hadn't gone through that. I never would have chosen it, but God used that experience to draw me closer to him than ever before."

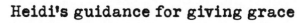

Heidi's guidance for giving grace

- Recognize that God tells us to forgive.
- Decide to obey that command.
- Don't wait until you feel like forgiving. Grace is a decision before it's an emotion.
- Remember that Jesus suffered even more to forgive you.
- Ask God to help your feelings match your actions of forgiveness.

BRAD — RECEIVING AND GIVING GRACE TO HIMSELF

Brad knew that he had brought all these problems on himself and his family. Was he forgiven by Christ? Yes, because God's grace covers even the worst sins. Was he forgiven by Heidi? Yes, because of her faithfulness to Christ's teachings, despite Brad's unfaithfulness to her.

But *experiencing* forgiveness and *feeling* liberated from shame and self-condemnation—those were far more difficult for Brad to achieve.

"You can experience God's grace only as much as you accept

full responsibility for what you've done," Brad said to me. "I needed to completely accept responsibility for what I had done so I could feel fully forgiven by God. Could I try to find excuses? Sure. But there have been people in far worse situations who have stayed faithful to Jesus. I didn't. I failed. I made the choices that I made. I can't point the finger at anyone else."

"Has it been a struggle to stop living in shame?"

He nodded. "Absolutely. Shame says that you didn't merely sin, but that you are an irredeemable sinner. Shame says that you're forever worthless as a person, that God can never use you again. I can't prevent those emotions from coming up, but I can choose to deal with them in a biblical way."

"What is a biblical way to deal with shame?"

"I remind myself that shame is not from God. What I did in the past was sinful, but it does not define who I am now, and it doesn't define my future. Romans 8:1 says, 'Therefore, there is now no condemnation for those who are in Christ Jesus.'

"I can have grief, but that's not shame. I can have a sense of loss, but that's not shame. I can regret the consequences of what I did, but that's not shame. The fact is, I hurt a lot of people. I can't undo that. I can feel remorse over it—and I do and I will—but the moment I begin feeling shame, I know that's the enemy at work.

"Christ paid for my sins on the cross. When I'm stuck in shame, that's me taking back on myself what Jesus took on himself. I'm ignoring what Christ accomplished. Jesus doesn't want me to stay punished. He took the punishment for what I did, and that gives me the freedom to move ahead with confidence and in grace.

"First John 1:9 says, 'If we confess our sins, he is faithful and just and will forgive us our sins and purify us from all unrighteousness.' But when I take on shame, then I'm saying that I'm not really purified, that the Cross was a failure, that Jesus' sacrifice for me wasn't enough.

"I need to get beyond the feelings of shame and focus on the *fact* that I'm free from condemnation, the *fact* that I've been made righteous in Christ, and on the *fact* that I've been purified. I want to live on those facts, not on shameful feelings."

"All of those *are* facts," I said, "but it's also a fact that God disciplines his children. After they sinned, Adam and Eve tried to avoid that by hiding from God. Was that a temptation for you?"

"Yeah, part of me wanted to flee," he replied. "I had to consciously open myself up to God's discipline, because I knew it was for my own good. Hebrews 12 says God's discipline produces holiness, righteousness, peace, and healing in us. Those were four things I desperately needed.

"If I tried to wiggle out of God's discipline by running from the consequences of my sin, then I'd be resisting what God wanted to accomplish in me. Only by facing my sin could God use it to change me for the better. The Bible warns that God's discipline isn't pleasant, but in the end, the changes God produces in our character are worth it. That was true for me.

"I remember a church official who called me. He went through the list of people in the Bible who sinned but God restored them and kept using them in ministry."

Brad's voice began to quake. "Man, I needed to hear that. He breathed hope into me. *Just maybe,* I thought, *God is big enough to take the mess I made and use it for his glory.*"

Brad's guidance for accepting grace

- Accept full responsibility for what you've done. No excuses.
- Confess your sin to God.
- Remind yourself that shame is not from God.
- Remember that God promises to forgive when you confess, and God keeps his promises.
- Don't try to wiggle out of the consequences of your sin. God is using those to teach you.
- Remember that God can use anything and anyone for his glory.

Brad's adultery will have consequences into the future. Certainly, the effects of sin should never be whitewashed. Nevertheless, Brad was right about this: God is big enough to redeem even the most hurtful of sins and to use the circumstances for good.

One day when Brad and Heidi were in counseling, the therapist told them, "Your marriage will emerge better because of all this."

Brad and Heidi laughed.

The counselor said, "Someday, you'll use this to help other people."

They laughed again.

"If you think we'll ever talk about this publicly," Heidi said, "you're dead wrong."

The counselor replied, "We'll see."

CAN YOU HELP US?

On a hot summer day in rural Ohio, more than 15,000 people were attending a Christian music festival. Between acts, hundreds of them would crowd into tents to hear speakers on a variety of topics.

The new pastor of a nearby church and his wife were teaching three sessions. They had moved to the area after a couple of years in South Carolina. Calling their ministry "Build Your Marriage," they talked about communication, intimacy, and conflict resolution. The subject of adultery wasn't on the agenda.

After one session, a couple came up to the speakers, Brad and Heidi. "I don't know if you can help us, but three months ago, my husband revealed that he had an affair," the woman said. "And I don't know if there's any hope for us."

Heidi couldn't hold back a sympathetic smile.

"Yes," Heidi assured her. "We can help." And the couple who had learned how to give and receive grace reached out to a couple who needed it.

The Case for Grace

CHAPTER NINE

The End (and a New Beginning) of the Story

i always wondered: would I cry when my father died?

After the argument in which my dad declared he didn't have enough love for me to fill his little finger, I stormed out of the house, determined never to return. I lived for two months in a small apartment nearly forty miles away as I worked as a reporter for a small daily newspaper. The publisher agreed to hire me beyond the summer. My future seemed set.

I never heard from my father, but my mother kept urging me to return. She would call and write to tell me my dad certainly couldn't have meant what he said. Finally, I did come home briefly, but my father and I never discussed the incident. I never brought it up, and neither did he.

From that point on, we were polite enough to each other, but we were never close. He paid for my college tuition, for which I never thanked him. He never wrote or visited, and he didn't come to my graduation. When I got married after my sophomore year at the University of Missouri, my parents hosted the reception, but my dad and I never had a heart-to-heart talk.

After graduation, I got a job as a newspaper reporter at the *Chicago Tribune*. After a while, I took a leave of absence to study at Yale Law School. I planned to return to the *Tribune* as legal editor.

A few days before my graduation, I settled into the school library and unfolded the *New York Times* for a leisurely morning of reading. I was already prepared for my final exams and was getting excited about returning to Chicago.

Then, my friend Howard appeared. I folded the newspaper and greeted him; he stared at me as if he had something urgent to say but couldn't find the right words.

"What's wrong?" I asked. He didn't answer, but somehow I knew. "My father died, right?"

He nodded, then led me to the privacy of a small alcove, where I sobbed inconsolably.

ALONE WITH MY FATHER

Before my father's wake began at the funeral parlor, I asked for some time alone in the room. I stood in front of the open casket for the longest time. A lifetime of thoughts tumbled through my mind. My emotions churned. There was nothing to say, and yet there was everything to say.

So many times in my life, I had told myself that the coldness between me and my dad was all his fault, not mine. *He's the one who should be apologizing to me*. Or pride got in my way. *Why should I go crawling to him?* Or sometimes I'd just put it off. *I can always handle that later*.

Finally, after a long period of silence, I managed to whisper the words I desperately wished I had spoken so many years earlier: "I'm sorry, Dad."

Sorry for the ways I had rebelled against him, lied to him, and

The Case for Grace

disrespected him over the years. Sorry for being ungrateful. Sorry for the bitterness I had allowed to poison my heart. For the first time, I admitted my share of the blame in our relationship.

Then came my last words to my father: "I forgive you." As best I could, I extended him grace — too late for our relationship, but in so many ways, liberating and life changing for me.

Over time, I found that nothing heals like grace.

UNEXPECTED WORDS

Soon business associates, neighbors, golfing buddies, and others arrived at the wake to express their sympathy to my mother and other members of the family. I sat by myself in a folding chair off to the side. I was dealing with deep and conflicted emotions and didn't feel like interacting with anyone.

One of my dad's business associates walked over and sat down beside me. "Are you Lee?" he asked.

"Yes, I am," I said. We shook hands.

"Well, it's great to finally meet you after hearing so much about you," he said. "Your dad could never stop talking about you. He was so proud of you and excited about what you're doing. Every time you'd have an article in the *Tribune*, he'd clip it and show it to everyone. When you went off to Yale — well, he was bursting with pride. He was always showing us pictures of your kids. He couldn't stop bragging about you. It's good to finally put a face with the name, because we heard your name a lot from your dad. 'Lee's doing this.' 'Lee's doing that.' 'Did you see Lee's article on the front page?' But then, I suppose you knew all that."

My mind reeled as I tried to conceal my astonishment. I couldn't help wondering what might have been different if those words had come to me directly from my dad.

When I became a follower of Jesus several years after my dad's death, I saw how different a relationship could be. Here, there was no concealing how my Father felt about me. The Bible shouted it over and over until I had to believe it. *God loves me. No matter how bad I am; no matter how good I am; no matter what. His grace is unending. I am his workmanship and his pride. He couldn't stand the thought of spending eternity without me in his family.*

And as God's grace utterly rocked my life — forgiving me, adopting me, and changing my life and my eternity — something else became clear: how awful it would be to withhold the news of that grace from others. How could I enjoy it myself but never pass it along to a world that is dying for it?

What if Michelle had never hugged Cody Huff? What if Luis Palau had never reached out to his son Andrew? What if the woman in the refugee camp had never revealed the meaning of the cross to Christopher LaPel?

> "[God] dispenses his goodness not with an eyedropper but a fire hydrant. Your heart is a Dixie cup, and his grace is the Mediterranean Sea. You simply can't contain it all. So let it bubble over. Spill out. Pour forth. 'Freely you have received, freely give.'"
>
> — MAX LUCADO[26]

Writing about my journey of grace in this book makes me want to share that grace all the more. That is the joyful task of every follower of Jesus. Someday may it be written about me on my tombstone: *He was so amazed by God's grace that he couldn't keep it to himself.*

READ IT HERE

WHAT THE BIBLE SAYS ABOUT GRACE

* And I will pour out on the house of David and the inhabitants of Jerusalem a spirit of grace and supplication. They will look on me, the one they have pierced, and they will mourn for him as one mourns for an only child, and grieve bitterly for him as one grieves for a firstborn son. — Zechariah 12:10

* And the child [Jesus] grew and became strong; he was filled with wisdom, and the grace of God was on him. — Luke 2:40

* The Word became flesh and made his dwelling among us. We have seen his glory, the glory of the one and only Son, who came from the Father, full of grace and truth. — John 1:14

* Out of his fullness we have all received grace in place of grace already given. — John 1:16

* For the law was given through Moses; grace and truth came through Jesus Christ. — John 1:17

* Now Stephen, a man full of God's grace and power, performed great wonders and signs among the people. — Acts 6:8

* When he arrived and saw what the grace of God had done, he was glad and encouraged them all to remain true to the Lord with all their hearts. — Acts 11:23

* When the congregation was dismissed, many of the Jews and devout converts to Judaism followed Paul and Barnabas, who talked with them and urged them to continue in the grace of God. — Acts 13:43

* So Paul and Barnabas spent considerable time there, speaking boldly for the Lord, who confirmed the message of his grace by enabling them to perform signs and wonders. — Acts 14:3

* We believe it is through the grace of our Lord Jesus that we are saved, just as they are. — Acts 15:11

* When Apollos wanted to go to Achaia, the brothers and sisters encouraged him and wrote to the disciples there to welcome him. When he arrived, he was a great help to those who by grace had believed. — Acts 18:27

* However, I consider my life worth nothing to me; my only aim is to finish the race and complete the task the Lord Jesus has given me — the task of testifying to the good news of God's grace. — Acts 20:24

* Now I commit you to God and to the word of his grace, which can build you up and give you an inheritance among all those who are sanctified. — Acts 20:32

* Through him we received grace and apostleship to call all the Gentiles to the obedience that comes from faith for his name's sake. — Romans 1:5

* To all in Rome who are loved by God and called to be his holy people: Grace and peace to you from God our Father and from the Lord Jesus Christ. — Romans 1:7

* And all are justified freely by his grace through the redemption that came by Christ Jesus. — Romans 3:24

* Therefore, the promise comes by faith, so that it may be by grace and may be guaranteed to all Abraham's offspring — not only to those who are of the law but also to those who have the faith of Abraham. He is the father of us all. — Romans 4:16

* But the gift is not like the trespass. For if the many died by the trespass of the one man, how much more did God's grace and the gift that came by the grace of the one man, Jesus Christ,

overflow to the many! Nor can the gift of God be compared with the result of one man's sin: The judgment followed one sin and brought condemnation, but the gift followed many trespasses and brought justification. For if, by the trespass of the one man, death reigned through that one man, how much more will those who receive God's abundant provision of grace and of the gift of righteousness reign in life through the one man, Jesus Christ! — Romans 5:15–17

* The law was brought in so that the trespass might increase. But where sin increased, grace increased all the more, so that, just as sin reigned in death, so also grace might reign through righteousness to bring eternal life through Jesus Christ our Lord. — Romans 5:20–21

* What shall we say, then? Shall we go on sinning so that grace may increase? By no means! We are those who have died to sin; how can we live in it any longer? Or don't you know that all of us who were baptized into Christ Jesus were baptized into his death? — Romans 6:1–3

* For sin shall no longer be your master, because you are not under the law, but under grace. What then? Shall we sin because we are not under the law but under grace? By no means! — Romans 6:14–15

* So too, at the present time there is a remnant chosen by grace. And if by grace, then it cannot be based on works; if it were, grace would no longer be grace. — Romans 11:5–6

* For by the grace given me I say to every one of you: Do not think of yourself more highly than you ought, but rather think of yourself with sober judgment, in accordance with the faith God has distributed to each of you. — Romans 12:3

* We have different gifts, according to the grace given to each of us. — Romans 12:6

* The God of peace will soon crush Satan under your feet. The grace of our Lord Jesus be with you. — Romans 16:20

* I always thank my God for you because of his grace given you in Christ Jesus. — 1 Corinthians 1:4

* By the grace God has given me, I laid a foundation as a wise builder, and someone else is building on it. But each one should build with care. — 1 Corinthians 3:10

* But by the grace of God I am what I am, and his grace to me was not without effect. No, I worked harder than all of them — yet not I, but the grace of God that was with me. — 1 Corinthians 15:10

* Now this is our boast: Our conscience testifies that we have conducted ourselves in the world, and especially in our relations with you, with integrity and godly sincerity. We have done so, relying not on worldly wisdom but on God's grace. — 2 Corinthians 1:12

* All this is for your benefit, so that the grace that is reaching more and more people may cause thanksgiving to overflow to the glory of God. — 2 Corinthians 4:15

* As God's co-workers we urge you not to receive God's grace in vain. — 2 Corinthians 6:1

* But since you excel in everything — in faith, in speech, in knowledge, in complete earnestness and in the love we have kindled in you — see that you also excel in this grace of giving. — 2 Corinthians 8:7

* For you know the grace of our Lord Jesus Christ, that though he was rich, yet for your sake he became poor, so that you through his poverty might become rich. — 2 Corinthians 8:9

* And in their prayers for you their hearts will go out to you, because of the surpassing grace God has given you. — 2 Corinthians 9:14

* But he said to me, "My grace is sufficient for you, for my power is made perfect in weakness." Therefore I will boast all the more gladly about my weaknesses, so that Christ's power may rest on me. — 2 Corinthians 12:9

The Case for Grace

* I am astonished that you are so quickly deserting the one who called you to live in the grace of Christ and are turning to a different gospel — which is really no gospel at all. Evidently some people are throwing you into confusion and are trying to pervert the gospel of Christ. — Galatians 1:6–7

* James, Cephas, and John, those esteemed as pillars, gave me and Barnabas the right hand of fellowship when they recognized the grace given to me. They agreed that we should go to the Gentiles, and they to the circumcised. — Galatians 2:9

* I do not set aside the grace of God, for if righteousness could be gained through the law, Christ died for nothing! — Galatians 2:21

* You who are trying to be justified by the law have been alienated from Christ; you have fallen away from grace. — Galatians 5:4

* For he chose us in him before the creation of the world to be holy and blameless in his sight. In love he predestined us for adoption to sonship through Jesus Christ, in accordance with his pleasure and will — to the praise of his glorious grace, which he has freely given us in the One he loves. In him we have redemption through his blood, the forgiveness of sins, in accordance with the riches of God's grace that he lavished on us. — Ephesians 1:4–8

* But because of his great love for us, God, who is rich in mercy, made us alive with Christ even when we were dead in transgressions — it is by grace you have been saved. And God raised us up with Christ and seated us with him in the heavenly realms in Christ Jesus, in order that in the coming ages he might show the incomparable riches of his grace, expressed in his kindness to us in Christ Jesus. For it is by grace you have been saved, through faith — and this is not from yourselves, it is the gift of God — not by works, so that no one can boast. — Ephesians 2:4–9

* I became a servant of this gospel by the gift of God's grace given me through the working of his power. Although I am less than the least of all the Lord's people, this grace was given me: to preach to the Gentiles the boundless riches of Christ, and to make plain to everyone the administration of this mystery, which for ages past was kept hidden in God, who created all things. — Ephesians 3:7–9

* But to each one of us grace has been given as Christ apportioned it. — Ephesians 4:7

* Grace to all who love our Lord Jesus Christ with an undying love. — Ephesians 6:24

* It is right for me to feel this way about all of you, since I have you in my heart and, whether I am in chains or defending and confirming the gospel, all of you share in God's grace with me. — Philippians 1:7

* In the same way, the gospel is bearing fruit and growing throughout the whole world — just as it has been doing among you since the day you heard it and truly understood God's grace. — Colossians 1:6

* Let your conversation be always full of grace, seasoned with salt, so that you may know how to answer everyone. — Colossians 4:6

* I, Paul, write this greeting in my own hand. Remember my chains. Grace be with you. — Colossians 4:18

* We pray this so that the name of our Lord Jesus may be glorified in you, and you in him, according to the grace of our God and the Lord Jesus Christ. — 2 Thessalonians 1:12

* May our Lord Jesus Christ himself and God our Father, who loved us and by his grace gave us eternal encouragement and good hope, encourage your hearts and strengthen you in every good deed and word. — 2 Thessalonians 2:16–17

* The grace of our Lord Jesus Christ be with you all. — 2 Thessalonians 3:18

* The grace of our Lord was poured out on me abundantly, along with the faith and love that are in Christ Jesus. — 1 Timothy 1:14

The Case for Grace

* To Timothy, my dear son: Grace, mercy and peace from God the Father and Christ Jesus our Lord.—2 Timothy 1:2

* He has saved us and called us to a holy life—not because of anything we have done but because of his own purpose and grace. This grace was given us in Christ Jesus before the beginning of time, but it has now been revealed through the appearing of our Savior, Christ Jesus, who has destroyed death and has brought life and immortality to light through the gospel.—2 Timothy 1:9–10

* You then, my son, be strong in the grace that is in Christ Jesus.—2 Timothy 2:1

* The Lord be with your spirit. Grace be with you all. —2 Timothy 4:22

* For the grace of God has appeared that offers salvation to all people.—Titus 2:11

* But when the kindness and love of God our Savior appeared, he saved us, not because of righteous things we had done, but because of his mercy. He saved us through the washing of rebirth and renewal by the Holy Spirit, whom he poured out on us generously through Jesus Christ our Savior, so that, having been justified by his grace, we might become heirs having the hope of eternal life.—Titus 3:4–7

* But we do see Jesus, who was made lower than the angels for a little while, now crowned with glory and honor because he suffered death, so that by the grace of God he might taste death for everyone.—Hebrews 2:9

* Let us then approach God's throne of grace with confidence, so that we may receive mercy and find grace to help us in our time of need.—Hebrews 4:16

* How much more severely do you think someone deserves to be punished who has trampled the Son of God underfoot, who has treated as an unholy thing the blood of the covenant that sanctified them, and who has insulted the Spirit of grace?—Hebrews 10:29

* See to it that no one falls short of the grace of God and that no bitter root grows up to cause trouble and defile many. — Hebrews 12:15

* Do not be carried away by all kinds of strange teachings. It is good for our hearts to be strengthened by grace, not by eating ceremonial foods, which is of no benefit to those who do so. — Hebrews 13:9

* But he gives us more grace. That is why Scripture says: "God opposes the proud but shows favor to the humble." — James 4:6

* Concerning this salvation, the prophets, who spoke of the grace that was to come to you, searched intently and with the greatest care, trying to find out the time and circumstances to which the Spirit of Christ in them was pointing when he predicted the sufferings of the Messiah and the glories that would follow. — 1 Peter 1:10–11

* Therefore, with minds that are alert and fully sober, set your hope on the grace to be brought to you when Jesus Christ is revealed at his coming. — 1 Peter 1:13

* Each of you should use whatever gift you have received to serve others, as faithful stewards of God's grace in its various forms. — 1 Peter 4:10

* And the God of all grace, who called you to his eternal glory in Christ, after you have suffered a little while, will himself restore you and make you strong, firm and steadfast. — 1 Peter 5:10

* With the help of Silas, whom I regard as a faithful brother, I have written to you briefly, encouraging you and testifying that this is the true grace of God. Stand fast in it. — 1 Peter 5:12

* Grace and peace be yours in abundance through the knowledge of God and of Jesus our Lord. — 2 Peter 1:2

* But grow in the grace and knowledge of our Lord and Savior Jesus Christ. To him be glory both now and forever! Amen. — 2 Peter 3:18

HELPFUL BOOKS ON GRACE

Blue, Ken, and Alden Swan. *The Gospel Uncensored*. WestBow Press, 2010.

Bridges, Jerry. *The Discipline of Grace*. NavPress, 1994.

Bridges, Jerry. *Transforming Grace*. NavPress, 2008.

Falsani, Cathleen. *Sin Boldly*. Zondervan, 2008.

Jung, Joanne, J. *Knowing Grace*. Biblica, 2011.

Lucado, Max. *Grace*. Thomas Nelson, 2012.

Lucado, Max. *In the Grip of Grace*. Thomas Nelson, 1996.

Manning, Brennan. *The Ragamuffin Gospel*. Multnomah, 1990.

Manning, Brennan, with John Blase. *All is Grace*. David C. Cook, 2011.

Oden, Thomas C. *The Transforming Power of Grace*. Abingdon Press, 1993.

Palau, Andrew. *The Secret Life of a Fool*. Worthy, 2012.

Smedes, Lewis B. *Shame and Grace*. HarperOne, 1993.

Stanley, Andy. *The Grace of God*. Thomas Nelson, 2010.

Swindoll, Charles. *The Grace Awakening*. Thomas Nelson, 1990.

Taunton, Larry Alex. *The Grace Effect*. Thomas Nelson, 2011.

Tchividjian, Tullian. *One Way Love*. David C. Cook, 2013.

Wilder, Lynn K. *Unveiling Grace*. Zondervan, 2013.

Wilhite, Jud, with Bill Taaffe. *Uncensored Grace*. Multnomah, 2009.

Yancey, Philip. *Vanishing Grace*. Zondervan, 2014.

Yancey, Philip. *What's So Amazing About Grace?* Zondervan, 1997.

ABOUT THE AUTHOR

Atheist-turned-Christian Lee Strobel, the former award-winning legal editor of the *Chicago Tribune*, is a *New York Times* best-selling author of more than twenty books. He serves as Professor of Christian Thought at Houston Baptist University and as a teaching pastor at Woodlands Church in Texas.

Described in the *Washington Post* as "one of the evangelical community's most popular apologists," Lee shared the Christian Book of the Year award in 2005 for a curriculum he coauthored with Garry Poole about the movie *The Passion of the Christ*. He also won Gold Medallions for *The Case for Christ*, *The Case for Faith*, and *The Case for a Creator*, all of which have been made into documentaries distributed by Lionsgate.

His latest works include *The Case for Christianity Answer Book*; his first novel, *The Ambition*; and *The Case for Christ Study Bible*, which features hundreds of notes and articles. His free e-newsletter, *Investigating Faith*, is available at http:// leestrobel.com/.

Lee was educated at the University of Missouri (Bachelor of Journalism degree) and Yale Law School (Master of Studies in Law degree). He was a journalist for fourteen years at the *Chicago Tribune* and other newspapers, winning Illinois' highest honor for public service journalism from United Press International. He also led a team that won UPI's top award for investigative reporting in Illinois.

After investigating the evidence for Jesus, Lee became a Christian in 1981. He joined the staff of Willow Creek Community Church in 1987 and later became a teaching pastor. He joined Saddleback Valley Community Church as a teaching pastor in 2000. He left

Saddleback to write books and host the national network TV program *Faith Under Fire.*

In addition, Lee taught First Amendment law at Roosevelt University. In recognition of the extensive research for his books, he was honored by Southern Evangelical Seminary with the conferring of a Doctor of Divinity degree in 2007.

Lee's other books include *The Case for the Real Jesus, Finding the Real Jesus, God's Outrageous Claims, The Case for Christmas, The Case for Easter, The Unexpected Adventure* (coauthored with Mark Mittelberg), and *Surviving a Spiritual Mismatch in Marriage*, which he wrote with his wife, Leslie Strobel.

Lee also coauthored the *Becoming a Contagious Christian* course, which has trained a million-and-a-half Christians on how to naturally and effectively talk with others about Jesus.

He has been interviewed on such national TV networks as ABC, Fox, PBS, and CNN, and his articles have appeared in a variety of periodicals, including the *Christian Research Journal, Marriage Partnership, Discipleship Journal, Decision*, and the online editions of the *Wall Street Journal* and *Newsweek*. He has been a recurring guest on the *Bible Answer Man* and *Focus on the Family* radio programs. He is a member of the Evangelical Philosophical Society.

Lee and Leslie have been married for forty-two years and live in Texas. Their daughter, Alison, is the author of six novels and coauthor (with her husband Daniel) of two books for children. Their son, Kyle, has written several books on Jonathan Edwards and on spiritual formation. With a Ph.D. in theology from the University of Aberdeen and two master's degrees, Kyle is a professor at the Talbot School of Theology at Biola University.

NOTES

1. See: Paul C. Vitz, *Faith of the Fatherless: The Psychology of Atheism* (Dallas: Spence, 1999). On p. 16, Vitz says, "Freud makes the simple and easily understandable claim that once a child or youth is disappointed in or loses respect for their earthly father, belief in a heavenly father becomes impossible. That a child's psychological representation of his father is intimately connected to his understanding of God was assumed by Freud and has been rather well developed by a number of psychologists, especially psychoanalysts. In other words, an atheist's disappointment in and resentment of his own father unconsciously justifies his rejection of God." Many psychologists have stressed that the relationship between a child and his father is one factor among several that can influence his or her conception of God. Interestingly, research by Vern L. Bengtson of the University of Southern California at Santa Barbara found that for religious transmission through generations, "having a close bond with one's father matters even more than a close relationship with one's mother," except in Judaism. But he said, "Fervent faith cannot compensate for a distant dad." He found that "a father who is an exemplar, a pillar of the church, but doesn't provide warmth and affirmation to his kid does not have kids who follow him in his faith." See Mark Oppenheimer, "Book Explores Ways Faith is Kept, or Lost, Over Generations," *New York Times*, January 31, 2014, and Vern L. Bengtson with Norella M. Putney and Susan Harris, *Families and Faith: How Religion Is Passed Down across Generations* (New York: Oxford University Press, 2014).

2. See Charles Chandler, "From Disbelief to Devotion," *Decision*, March 2014.

3. All interviews are edited for conciseness, clarity, and content. Stephanie Fast's website is http://www.stephaniefast.org/. She tells her story in her book *She Is Mine* (Aloha, OR.: D&S Publishing, 2014).

4. Paraphrase of a part of Psalm 10:14.

5. Among the books in which he shares parts of his story are Jud Wilhite with Bill Taaffe, *Uncensored Grace* (Colorado Springs: Multnomah, 2008); Jud Wilhite, *Uncensored Truth* (Corona, CA: Ethur, 2010); Jud Wilhite, *Pursued: God's Divine Obsession with You* (New York: FaithWords, 2013); Jud Wilhite, *Throw It Down: Leaving Behind Behaviors and Dependencies That Hold You Back* (Grand Rapids, MI: Zondervan, 2011); and Jud Wilhite, *The God of Yes* (New York: Faith Words, 2014).

6. Philip Yancey, *What's So Amazing About Grace?*, (Grand Rapids, MI: Zondervan, 1997), 70.

7. *The Guiness Book of World Records 1999,* p. 23.

8. Nic Dunlop, *The Lost Executioner* (New York: Walker, 2006), 189.

9. David Chandler, *Voices from S-21* (Berkeley: University of California Press, 1999), vii.

10. Chandler, *Voices From S-21*, 3.

11. Dunlop, *Lost Executioner*, 19.

12. Chandler, *Voices from S-21*, 6.

13. Dunlop, *Lost Executioner*, 23.

14. Duch's given name has been variously reported in articles and books. Christopher LaPel provided me with a photocopy of Duch's own writing, however, in which he clearly spells out his name as Kaing Guek Eav.

15. Seth Mydans, "'70's Torturer in Cambodia Now Doing God's Work," *New York Times*, May 2, 1999.

16. Mary Murphy, "Is There Anything God Can't Forgive?" *Purpose-Driven Magazine*, February 21, 2012.

17. Ibid.

18. See Dunlop, *Lost Executioner*, 254–62.

19. Dunlop describes their meeting with Duch in Dunlop, *Lost Executioner*, 267–78. Thayer recounts the experience at "Nate Thayer Profile," Nate Thayer, http://natethayer.typepad.com.

20. Adrienne S. Gaines, "Notorious Cambodian Killer Seeks Forgiveness," *Charisma*, April 2, 1999.

21. "Cambodia," *U.S. Department of State*, http://www.state.gov/j/drl/rls/irf/2010/148861.htm.

22. Murphy, "Is There Anything God Can't Forgive?"

23. See Luis Palau Association, http://www.palau.org/about/leadership-team/item/luis-palau.

24. See http://www.palau.org/.

25. To avoid clues to the woman's identity, I have left out certain details of their relationship.

26. Max Lucado, *Grace* (Nashville, TN: Thomas Nelson, 2012), 192, citing Matthew 10:8.

The Case for Christ — Student Edition

A Journalist's Personal Investigation of the Evidence for Jesus

Lee Strobel with Jane Vogel

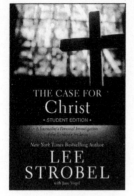

There's little question that he actually lived. But miracles? Rising from the dead? Some of the stories you hear about him sound like just that — stories. A reasonable person would never believe them, let alone the claim that he's the only way to God!

But a reasonable person would also make sure that he or she understood the facts before jumping to conclusions. That's why Lee Strobel — an award-winning legal journalist with a knack for asking tough questions — decided to investigate Jesus for himself. An atheist, Strobel felt certain his findings would bring Christianity's claims about Jesus tumbling down like a house of cards.

He was in for the surprise of his life. Join him as he retraces his journey from skepticism to faith. You'll consult expert testimony as you sift through the truths that history, science, psychiatry, literature, and religion reveal. Like Strobel, you'll be amazed at the evidence — how much there is, how strong it is, and what it says.

The facts are in. What will your verdict be in *The Case for Christ*?

Available in stores and online!

The Case for Faith Student Edition

A Journalist Investigates
the Toughest Objections to
Christianity

Lee Strobel with Jane Vogel

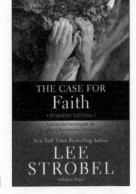

Lee Strobel knows how important it is to find
answers that ring true. With his background as
an award-winning legal journalist, asking tough questions has been his
business. And while his search for the truth convinced Lee that Jesus
is real, it also confronted him with some particularly knotty, gut-level
questions about Christianity. Why is there suffering? Doesn't science
disprove miracles? What about hell—and the millions who've never
heard of Jesus? Is God unjust? They're the kind of conundrums that
can—and have—blocked people's faith.

They don't have to block yours. Join Lee in a fascinating journey of
discovery. You'll gain powerful insights that will reshape your understanding of the Bible. And you'll read true stories of people whose
experiences demonstrate that faith in Jesus not only make excellent
sense, but a life-changing difference.

Available in stores and online!

The Case for the Real Jesus Student Edition

A Journalist Investigates Current Challenges to Christianity

Lee Strobel with Jane Vogel

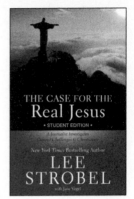

Just about everyone you ask has an opinion about Jesus. Some believe he was the Son of God, while others question his existence altogether. Some believe he lived, but that he was merely a good man. Today, scientists and other people are making statements that can make it difficult to know what to believe. So how can you know who the real Jesus was (and is)—especially when so many people are working to prove him to be a fake or a fraud? That's what Lee Strobel wanted to know.

As a former journalist—and a former atheist—Lee went on an investigative journey to discover the real Jesus, one that took him across the continent and into the homes of today's most prominent experts on Christian history. He found all the evidence he needed to believe that the Jesus is indeed the Risen Savior.

Join Lee's investigation and discover the truth about Jesus for yourself. After you've seen all the evidence, you'll know for certain who the real Jesus is, and you'll be able to help others know him as well.

Available in stores and online!

ZONDERVAN®
.com

The Case for a Creator Student Edition

A Journalist Investigates Scientific Evidence That Points Toward God

Lee Strobel with Jane Vogel

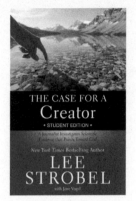

In *The Case for a Creator—Student Edition*, best-selling author and former atheist Lee Strobel and popular writer Jane Vogal take younger readers on a remarkable investigation into the origin of the universe, interviewing many of the world's renown scientists and following their evidence wherever it leads.

Their findings—presented in the third blockbuster "Case" book student edition—offer the most compelling scientific proof ever for intelligent design. Perfect for youth groups and young people eager to rebut the Darwinian and naturalistic views taught so commonly in schools.

Available in stores and online!